"Extraordinary Solitude shows that Jesus' redemptive love—and His plan for every life—can withstand, and even thrive in, the hardest of situations, as long as He finds a heart willing to let Him in. Steven conveys that this can be a process, as Jesus forms our lives into ones like His. But He is relentless in doing so, creating beauty from ashes, giving us all we need, and all the while being close by our side. Jesus can turn any life into an adventure. How He did that with Steven will bring hope to many."

Randy Fisk, author;
The Presence, Power and Heart of God

"As a podcast host, I've interviewed over 700 guests on my show; so, I know every man has a unique story. But then there are some certain men whose stories test, challenge, and strengthen others' faith. That's Steven Snook; if he wasn't alive to tell his story, no one would ever believe it. I am thrilled that he decided to write this book, so others could understand the true power of God and His divine purpose and plan for all our lives."

Dr. Joe Martin, host of *Real Men Connect*, the #1 Christian Men's Podcast on Apple Podcasts, RealMenConnect.com

"It has been said the most powerful way to put ideas into the world is through a story. Steven's story shouts to the world, "There is a kind God in heaven who never stops pursuing His sons and daughters," and reminds us that Jesus Himself steps into prison cells and frees the captives from the inside out. The story of redemption and meaning out of brokenness and suffering washes into every chapter. Hope is embodied within each recounting of the impossible being not only possible but a lived-in reality. If you have ever wondered if God still performs miracles or if transformation and restoration are true, open the pages of this book and find yourself immersed in a story that will forever carry an impact and, very possibly, settle the wondering within your heart. This story is the story of the gospel in our day."

Maureen Gray, ICF coach, MTS certified, emotional wholeness coach, speaker & producer

Extraordinary Solitude

Prison, Razor Blades & Jesus

Steven Snook

EXTRAORDINARY SOLITUDE

Extraordinary Solitude:
Prison, Razor Blades & Jesus

Published by Jesus Speaks LLC

First edition. Copyright © 2023 by Steven Snook.

The information contained in this book is the intellectual property of Steven Snook and is governed by United States and international copyright laws. All rights reserved. No part of this publication, either text or image, may be used for any purpose other than personal use. Therefore, reproduction, modification, storage in a retrieval system, or retransmission, in any form or by any means, electronic, mechanical, or otherwise, for reasons other than personal use, except for brief quotations for reviews or articles and promotions, is strictly prohibited without prior written permission by the publisher.

Events, locales, and conversations included in this book are from the author's memories and conversations with family and friends. To maintain anonymity, in some instances, the author has changed the names of individuals, places, identifying characteristics, and details of his journey.

All Scripture quotations, unless otherwise indicated, are taken from the Holy Bible, New King James Version®. Copyright © 1982 by Thomas Nelson. Used by permission. All rights reserved.

Cover design by Michael Stubbs

Interior design by Evelyn J. Wagoner

ISBN 979-8-9867589-0-9

www.JesusSpeaksLLC.com

JesusSpeaksLLC@gmail.com

ExtraordinarySolitude@gmail.com

EXTRAORDINARY SOLITUDE

To the Holy Spirit

—the most important Person on earth

and

to Aunt Marsha

who endured sorrow upon sorrow, yet opened
her loving heart to two abandoned brothers
and gave them a home

EXTRAORDINARY SOLITUDE

EXTRAORDINARY SOLITUDE

> "You are of God, little children,
> and have overcome them,
> because He who is in you is greater
> than he who is in the world."
> (1 John 4:4)

EXTRAORDINARY SOLITUDE

Contents

Foreword i

Introduction iii

PART ONE—CHAOS

Chapter 1 Longing for a Home 9
Chapter 2 From Bad to Worse 13
Chapter 3 The Violence Escalates 21
Chapter 4 An Internal Contradiction 33
Chapter 5 The Deepening Darkness 41
Chapter 6 Hitting Bottom 55

PART TWO—REBORN

Chapter 7   Lost and Found 69
Chapter 8   Two Steps Forward, One Step Back 83
Chapter 9   A Divine Connection 95
Chapter 10 The Valley of the Shadow 107

PART THREE—RETURN

Chapter 11 Heading for Home 123
Chapter 12 Going Deeper, Growing Stronger 127
Chapter 13 Evidence of Baptism & Tongues 145
Chapter 14 Hearing the Voice of the Lord 153
Chapter 15 In My Dreams 159
Chapter 16 The Lord Speaks Through Visions 169

PART FOUR--REVELATION

Chapter 17	The Door to the Supernatural	179
Chapter 18	Ministering to the Brethren	185
Chapter 19	Following God, Leading Others	189
Chapter 20	Answered Prayers for Healing	203
Chapter 21	Led by Dreams	209
Chapter 22	A New Beginning	213
Chapter 23	The Longest Fast	219
Chapter 24	Prison, Razor Blades & Jesus	233
Chapter 25	Living the Life	239

Afterword 243

Acknowledgments 245

Special Acknowledgments 247

Appendix—Letters to José 249

About the Cover 275

About the Author 277

Foreword

The Bible says that God's arms "are not too short" to reach into any situation or into any person's heart. Steven Snook is the real-life evidence of the truth of that statement. His life is a journey of pain and struggle, victory and triumph, human failure and God's amazing grace. Read this powerful book as a testimony. It is a testimony to God's redemptive love, and a testimony to the amazing grace that reaches into the deepest, darkest places to rescue the lost lambs of God.

Whether you are a seasoned Christian who is hungering for more power of the Holy Spirit, or you are in a place far from God right now, God's arms are reaching out to you through this book. Whether you are sitting in your living room at ease or sitting in a prison cell, somehow this book has made its way to you. Pay attention: this book is not a coincidence! It is God reaching out to you. His arms are not too short! Let Him speak to you through the testimony that lies within these pages. Let God take you on a journey to places that may be foreign to you. Places that may at times make you uncomfortable. Or maybe places you are very familiar with and you will even say, "This is me." Let God show you the love that conquers all things, and the power that works miracles in our lives. Steven Snook has walked in all of it. Listen to him as he shares his story.

God has already acted: If you're holding this book in your hand, then God has reached you.

My prayer for you is that you will be one of hundreds of bold testimonies that will come out of this book. And my prayer is that those testimonies will spark hundreds more. And I pray there will be a holy fire of thousands of bold warriors for Christ in the church because a bold man picked up half a pencil in solitary confinement and began to write the story of God's redemptive love: "I was born on December 5, 1976..."

Thank you, Steven. Your boldness and persistence in following Jesus and in writing this book is a tremendous gift to the Body of Christ.

Pastor Tom Eckhardt
Bradley Epworth Church
Peoria, IL

Introduction

> I will praise You, for I am
> fearfully and wonderfully made;
> Marvelous are Your works,
> And that my soul knows very well.
> My frame was not hidden from You,
> When I was made in secret,
> And skillfully wrought in the
> lowest parts of the earth.
> Your eyes saw my substance,
> being yet unformed.
> And in Your book they all were written,
> The days fashioned for me,
> When as yet there were none of them.
> (Psalm 139:14-16)

A famous song tells us that the beginning is a very good place to start. That may be true in general, but I've learned that God knew me *before* I was formed, *before* I drew my first breath. Though I didn't recognize His fingerprints until many years had passed, when I look back on all I've experienced—both good and decidedly evil—I can see the hand of God on my life.

In 2001, I learned the circumstances of my birth and early years from my mother. We didn't know each other well and had only met five or six times my entire life. We cried together as she shared her story and mine. I had recently been released from prison... the first time. I'm certain that if we explored my mother's birth and perhaps her mother's birth and even further back, we would discover generation after generation of poverty, abuse, death, and curses.

My early years were filled with chaos and brutality—not the best building blocks for a young child's life. But that's not the whole story. As a long-term prisoner, I walked daily through the valley of the shadow of death. Years later, made new by the blood of Jesus and filled with the Holy Spirit, I learned to take authority over demons and experienced the gifts of the Holy Spirit. But first, to truly understand why God gives so much more grace and mercy than we could ever deserve, travel with me down the road of death and destruction and revisit the horrifying events of my life. We are a people that must experience God's power and presence to truly be alive. My prayer is that you will read my story with the understanding and knowledge that the Light has overcome the darkness.

In addition to decades of turmoil and violence in many forms, my life has also been filled with bizarre

EXTRAORDINARY SOLITUDE

and amazing accounts of God's love and mercy. There are tales of tragedy and heartbreak. Miracles and Jesus. About madness and demons. About suicides and murders. About lives risked to save others. And about the Holy Spirit at work today. My story centers on a supernatural Jesus who is alive and who called me from the womb. He continues to work miracles and give us power over demons and disease.

The how and the why of a story are always in the details. Stay with me. Surprises are on the way.

Let's begin . . . at the beginning.

EXTRAORDINARY SOLITUDE

Part One
Chaos

EXTRAORDINARY SOLITUDE

Chapter 1

Longing for a Home

*"Children do learn what they live.
Then they grow up to live what they've learned."*
(Dorothy Nolte)

Birth to Age 6

I was born on December 5, 1976, to Nancy, a fifteen-year-old girl who was already mother to a seventeen-month-old son. She had no parental guidance. No husband. No boyfriend. No support system of any kind. Truly alone and lost, she didn't know what to do when she found herself pregnant a second time. She was so poor, she couldn't afford to rent a television while in the hospital. The stranger who shared the room offered to pay for the TV, and Nancy gladly accepted. As they chatted, my mother asked her roommate what she thought would be a good name for a little boy. She answered, "Steven." And that became my name.

EXTRAORDINARY SOLITUDE

Two years later, worse-than-welfare poor, my mother left me and my brother, Chopper, by the roadside and then called the police. Desperate and exhausted, she didn't know what else to do. Chopper and I were taken to a foster home. While I cannot remember the good people who took us in, I'm convinced they were Christians. I'll explain why later.

We saw Chopper's father, a deadbeat who had no interest in his son, only a few times during our childhood. Though I was always told he was my dad, everyone knew Chopper and I were half-brothers, sharing only a mother. Chopper's Aunt Marsha didn't care about our parentage. She was young, married, and childless. Driving to Hampton, Virginia, along with great-aunt Liz and great-uncle George, Aunt Marsha relocated my brother, leaving me behind with our foster parents. But she wanted to keep us together and returned a few months later to take custody of me as well, bringing me to join Chopper in Illinois.

Not yet three years old, I recall sitting in the back of a car behind the passenger seat, my little legs dangling above the floorboard. As I stared at my swinging feet, I sang the alphabet song for the three adults. Though I was alone with strangers, I wasn't sad or afraid. I just concentrated on the ABCs.

Aunt Marsha, a petite brunette with a soft heart, lived with her husband, Bill, who was ex-military, big, and hot-tempered. From appearances, they were an all-American couple. Our new home was in rural

EXTRAORDINARY SOLITUDE

Illinois with only a half-dozen neighbors scattered within a mile radius. There weren't many kids for us to play with, but Chopper and I had each other. While my memories of this time are few, they seem quite remarkable to me and are relevant to events later in my life.

One warm, sunny day when I was about four, I ran across the yard toward my brother and his friend, eager to share an exciting discovery. I had found a half-full gas can used to fill the lawnmower, and I could hardly wait to start a fire. At that moment, Aunt Marsha came to the backdoor and saw me running with the gas can. She hauled me into the house and spanked me before sending me back out to play. What would have happened had I managed to start that fire?

When I was in kindergarten, we seemed to be constantly transferring back and forth between schools. I don't know why we went from one school to another and then back to the same school again. During that time period, Marsha and I were driving in the pouring rain. The country roads were covered with thousands and thousands of nightcrawlers. We ran them over and continued on our way home.

Another memory from that period of my young life is one I have often pondered as an adult and still don't understand. One stormy night, I sat on Marsha's lap in our front room. As I stared at the woman who would raise me through childhood, Bill crossed the room and punched her in the face. Blood streamed from a cut above her eye. And Marsha had finally had enough. We moved in with her parents, and they became my grandma and grandpa for the rest of my life.

Chapter 2

From Bad to Worse

"Each day of our lives we make deposits in the memory banks of our children."
(Charles R. Swindoll)

Ages 7 to 10

Within a year, Marsha met Chuck. He had only one leg and used crutches. We moved to Florida to live with him. Before long, Chuck became abusive, hitting me and Chopper. Marsha took us back to live with Grandma and Grandpa after a few months.

While she made bad choices when it came to men, Marsha always did her best for Chopper and me. She raised us, though we weren't her own, and eventually gave birth to her own son. Having only a ninth-grade education, she worked her entire life as a waitress. She went to work at five in the morning, never missing a day, while raising sons and dealing with abusive, alcoholic husbands.

EXTRAORDINARY SOLITUDE

Before long, Marsha met Larry, a large man who had been a boxer in the US Army. He and Marsha were married and moved to the south side of Danville, Illinois. They purchased a dilapidated, two-bedroom house with plastic covering the windows. I considered Larry to be my father from then on. When he was sober, he was a good person, a good dad. But he was a severe alcoholic who drank straight, hard liquor. He was a maniac when he drank. He didn't work and, in retrospect, I think he refused to get a job. Perhaps he thought it was useless as he would eventually fall off the wagon and get fired.

While Larry taught me how to fight like a man, how to hunt and fish, he was by far the most verbally abusive person I've ever met. He spewed hateful, destructive, hurtful things. Though he wasn't physically abusive to Marsha, Chopper and I were fair game. He would show up drunk at our football games and get thrown out of the stands. Once he tried to strangle my grandfather with a phone cord. He shot our fish tank with a 12-gauge shotgun—in the front room of our house. Another time, he shot an arrow from a compound bow into the kitchen door.

During Larry's worst drunken rampages, Marsha, Chopper, and I would stay with Grandma and Grandpa. While this move should have protected me, it brought on a new stage of pain that included sexual abuse. This is difficult to discuss, but I can't leave out the darkest parts of my story. Not all molested women turn out to be strippers, but almost every stripper has been molested. The same is true with child molesters. Not all those that have been molested become child molesters themselves, but almost every child molester was molested as a child. I believe this pattern is true because the foul spirit of lust and perversion is transferred to that child when they were abused. Psychology may disagree, but statistics show a direct correlation.

    I was molested by Damian, Chopper's half-brother, a teenager who was supposed to be my half-brother, too. The abuse didn't take place over an extended period, and I only remember three specific instances. On one occasion, we had moved back in with Larry, and Damian came to visit. Marsha and Larry had gone out. Damian sat on my bed and asked if I remembered what we used to do at my grandma's house. Did I want to do that again? How sick is that? He asked me, an eight-year-old boy, if I wanted to be molested again. With all the courage I could muster, I looked him in the eye and said no. I walked out of the room, out of the house. I don't know what would have happened as he was so much bigger and stronger than I. But I didn't have to find out. The moment I walked out the front door, Marsha pulled into the driveway, and I was saved again.

    I imagined how wonderful it would be if Chopper and I could be handcuffed together. We would never be separated, and I would be safe. We shared the same room and had bunk beds, but being handcuffed to my brother would have been true protection for me.

One night, while lying on the top bunk, I began thinking about life in a way a child should not be thinking, and I started to cry. Unable to stop, I went to Marsha and Larry's bedroom and, in tears, told them what had been happening to me. I told them everything. Larry didn't speak, but Marsha said it couldn't be true and I was a liar. She sent me back to bed, and we never discussed the issue again.

A bit of light did enter my life when I was in third grade. The schools in our district gave a series of tests to all the students. We weren't told what the tests were for beforehand, but a letter was sent to my house when the results came in. This may have been the only letter from school that wasn't about my being involved in some sort of trouble. They wanted to test me further to see if I qualified for new programs that were going to be implemented in our district. Marsha was confused. The program was called the MATS, and she thought it had something to do with an actual mat. She took me to take more tests.

At that time in our household, we didn't listen to the news on television. We didn't read the newspapers. There were no discussions about current events, no help with homework—nothing of any sort on an educational level. But I somehow did well on those tests, and the program wanted me. Who knew

EXTRAORDINARY SOLITUDE

that I would be considered a "smart" kid, and I would be included in a program in which most of the students were from wealthy families.

A special small bus picked me up for school each morning. I'm sure I learned a lot, but I mostly remember the field trips and learning to play chess, a skill which would play a major role later in life. Sadly, I was only in the program for 4th and 5th grades. Before I began sixth grade, Marsha and Larry decided I, at 10 years old, could decide for myself where I wanted to go to school. Of course, I chose to go to school with my friends. Not the wisest choice.

Family Photo 1985—(left to right) Steven, Aunt Marsha, L.J., Uncle Larry, Chopper

While we were again living at Grandma and Grandpa's house, during one of Larry's crazy episodes, I wandered down to the park where I played youth football. Something was going on. Lots of people crowded a large field and, curious, I decided to check it out. A beautiful girl started a conversation with me. She was probably five years older than I, but I fell in love instantly. All she talked about was Jesus. I was so enthralled I would have said yes to anything she asked. I must have agreed to something, because I started riding to church with her and her parents.

Before long, I was water baptized and realized the girl was only interested in converting me. I never went back to church after being baptized, but I do believe a seed was planted during that time. Looking back, I realize Jesus always had a hedge of protection around me.

Around the time I turned nine, Marsha became pregnant. During the final months of her pregnancy, someone decided that it would be wonderful if Chopper and I visited our biological mother in Virginia. Apparently, our mom had once traveled to Illinois in an attempt to retrieve me and Chopper, but we didn't remember her. She believed we were happy, so she decided to leave us in Illinois.

Chopper and I flew to Virginia on our own. Our mother picked us up at the airport and took us home with her. On one of our first nights there, an older couple visited us. It turns out they were the loving people who had taken us in when we were infants. I remember how nice they were and how their love just seemed to be part of their personalities, which is why I believe they were Christians. Again, God's hand on me from the very beginning.

EXTRAORDINARY SOLITUDE

A few days later our mother ran off with a boyfriend, leaving us with her mother.

Chopper and I sat together in the front room of an unfamiliar house, scared and uncertain, the situation a nightmare. Our mother's mom, a grandmother we had never met, came in and told us to be quiet. Apparently, her husband wasn't happy we were there and had punched her in the mouth. She pulled her upper lip away from the gum to show us where it had been split open and was bleeding.

Picking up the telephone, she called our mom and begged her to come back and get us. But she refused. She was going to Florida with her boyfriend. Frustrated, our grandmother handed the phone to me and Chopper.

"Cry for your mother," she urged in a loud whisper.

And cry we did—sobbing and pleading until Mom relented. She came to get us, her new boyfriend in tow.

Chopper and I spent summer break with our mother in Florida, but our time there is mostly a blur. I do remember Mom ran off here and there, and I smoked marijuana for the first time.

When we were sent back to Illinois, I was so eaten up with chigger bites that fingernail polish remover had to be applied to my testicles daily. And there was a surprise waiting for us. Marsha had given birth to L.J., our little brother. He would soon become

EXTRAORDINARY SOLITUDE

my best friend and my only companion. A heartbreaking event was on the horizon: the day Chopper ran away.

Chapter 3

The Violence Escalates

"The greatest battles of life are fought out daily in the silent chambers of the soul."
(David O. McKay)

Ages 11 to 13

Chopper and I were star athletes, and sports began to play a huge role in our lives. Football was my game of preference, while Chopper was more into baseball. He was the best baseball player in his age group in a city of 40,000. We played on the same team one year, but, because of our age difference, he moved up to the next league without me. After my birthday, I advanced to his league, and we played together again, practicing in our yard every free moment we could find. Age groupings were different in football, so we were always on separate teams. I was an absolute terror on the football field and become known as a ferocious hitter throughout the city.

EXTRAORDINARY SOLITUDE

Neither Chopper nor I were taller than 5'10." While we were both skinny with wiry frames, we were meaner and more aggressive than the other kids. We weren't bullies, but we were what I like to call "bully busters." We had learned to be tough from Uncle Larry and from fighting each other. Chopper and I had some of the most brutal fights you can imagine. He was older, bigger, and stronger, but I would never give up. He would have to cripple or kill me to win, and he knew it. We always fought to a draw.

Uncle Larry made it clear we were never to fight at school, until the day two kids jumped Chopper at junior high school and knocked half his front tooth off. We had a family meeting in the front room of our little shack, and Larry announced a new set of rules. If anyone touched us or so much as laid a finger on us, we had a green light to retaliate.

The Ultimate Fighting Championship (UFC) was not yet on the scene. But Larry had taught us a style of fighting—with punches, chokes, kicks, and knees—that the average street fighter hadn't been exposed to. He also equipped us with the ultimate weapon: a mindset to never stop fighting until the opponent was knocked out or choked out. I shake my head today when I look back at my life. Who teaches a young kid to fight like that?

Except for one draw, I was undefeated in these street fights. As I had been taught, I never gave up even when I was badly hurt. I've had too many hand fractures and broken noses to count. My jaw has been broken and wired shut. My teeth have been knocked loose. I've had stitches behind my ear, stitches across my forehead, and smaller injuries that still required stitches. On one occasion, my left eye was knocked loose in the socket, and I had to wear a metal patch for a month.

When Chopper and I visited our friend Ryan in a nearby town, I was challenged to a fight by some kids who were training in a dojo. As the big brother, Chopper gave his permission even though the boys were older than I. I still have no idea why we were fighting. We didn't know each other. My reputation as a fighter had spread to that community.

The first fight was held in someone's backyard. A large kid with an entourage approached me, and the fight was on. It lasted about thirty seconds, standard for a street brawl. He was a bloody mess, and I was still going at him hard. No one was willing to jump in and stop the fight, except, unbelievably, his girlfriend.

I was challenged later that same day by the boy's friend who was even bigger. Chopper wouldn't consent and said I needed rest, but we rescheduled the fight for later that evening. After eating dinner at Ryan's house, Chopper and I walked to the new meeting place alone and were surprised to find a large crowd. This was their turf, and it seemed like the entire city had shown up to support their fighter.

EXTRAORDINARY SOLITUDE

The spectators were mostly teens, and I was only 12 years old. My opponent was already there, sparring with his older brother. The onlookers crowded around, some sitting on tables to watch. When we squared off, he instantly hit me with a snap kick right in the throat. I took a slight step back, then roared in throwing a series of punches. It got ugly very fast. He soon gave up, but his brother yelled at him to keep fighting. He refused and took off running, his brother in hot pursuit, still trying to get him to continue fighting.

They never came back.

As you can see, street fighting was a major part of my youth. When I was a teenager, I got my first tattoo on my right arm—a rooster wearing boxing gloves.

* * *

I experienced my first true brush with death when I was twelve. Chopper and I, along with a couple of Chopper's friends, were sledding near a river in the forest by our house. Sean and Eddie were brothers, older than we. Sean would one day die from a Fentanyl overdose. After sledding, we took a walk to the nearby Vermillion River, which can be swift moving when the water is up or the dam is open. That day a thin layer of ice covered the river. One of the brothers dared me to crawl out on a fallen tree limb in the river. I took the dare. I climbed on the tree limb but began to slip. The icy current pulled my legs sideways, and my arms and hands lost their grip. I glanced in desperation to the river's edge to see Chopper and Sean laughing, not sensing that I was in danger of being carried downstream and under the ice in water that was over my head. As I was pulled under by the current, I knew I was moments from death. Eddie finally saw the fear on my face. He scrambled toward me and stretched out his hand. Reaching toward me as far as he could, he yelled for me to grab his hand. I lost my grip, but he pulled me, cold, drenched, and sputtering, to the shore.

  This story may seem a bit insignificant, but I, again, see the hand of God in my life. Only He could orchestrate what followed.

  When I was fourteen, I walked through that same forest with a friend of mine. It was late February and still cold, and we were looking for deer antlers. After hiking for a mile or so, we came to the railroad tracks near the closed-down General Motors plant. A group of kids played beside a run-off pond covered with a sheet of ice. It was as though history was going to repeat itself right in front of my eyes. On a dare, one kid ran to the center of the pond. The ice beneath him seemed to undulate and then splintered, plunging him into the depths. I didn't stop to think. Acting on pure instinct, I ran out to the middle of the pond to try to save him. When I got close, the ice broke beneath my feet, and I joined him in the freezing water. I grabbed him by the shoulder, but he didn't know how to swim and started kicking and flailing. I held him tight with one arm and broke away the ice with the other arm. We managed to get closer and closer to the bank, but I still couldn't touch bottom. His brother ran around the side of the bank and held out a stick. I put the stick in the boy's hand, and he was pulled to safety. I then heaved myself onto the shore.

Ten years later I ran into that young man. I would have never recognized him, but he walked up to me and thanked me for saving his life. He asked if he could do anything for me. I couldn't think of anything and was surprised to see the disappointment on his face. He was a garbage man and would like to do anything he could. I pointed to an old bathtub in a junk pile near my garage and asked if it would fit in the garbage truck. It was too big, but he said he would come back later and get it himself. I told him it wasn't necessary, but the bathtub was gone the next morning. I never saw him or the bathtub again.

Grades six through eight were filled with fights at school, along with a lot of suspensions. Thankfully, my grades were always just good enough to overcome the time lost. During suspensions, I spent hours hunting or fishing, often with Larry. It was usually just the two of us, as Chopper never had much success. We would each fish in the same fishing spot, and I would reel them in, and he wouldn't catch any. Sometimes we hunted in the exact same area on back-to-back days, and I would kill my limit of squirrels, while he didn't shoot even one.

During this time, Larry and I became very close, almost like father and son. Alcohol ruined everything. Larry could never stop drinking for long. We would enjoy three fishing trips and then, on the fourth, he would get totally wasted. As I mentioned earlier, he was a mean and violent drunk. If we were out on the boat, I would have to endure his verbal abuse for hours at a time.

Hunting was no different. It made no sense to me, but I can now see that he was bound by demons. He once told me, in a serious moment, that if I was ever in a situation where something or someone was trying to hurt me and there was no way of escape, I should call on the name of Jesus and rebuke the enemy in His name. I am still amazed, thirty years later, that those words came out of that man's mouth.

During that same time period, an extremely traumatic incident occurred. Chopper and I were throwing the football around in the yard. As the sun was setting, he looked me in the eye and said he was running away. He wanted me to stay outside for a while but to tell Marsha and Larry, when they asked where he was, that he had taken off. He turned and walked away. Away from all the pain and all the abuse. Just like that, he was gone . . . and he stayed gone. I found out later that he had jumped trains like a hobo, traveling to Virginia and as far away as California.

EXTRAORDINARY SOLITUDE

After Chopper left, I worked with a boxing trainer for a while, riding my bike to the gym to train and work out. I grew stronger, perfecting my stance, increasing my stamina, and learning to extend my reach. I had no doubt my improved skills would be put to good use at some point, but I had no idea how soon that occasion would come.

Family Photo 1989—Uncle Larry, Steven, Aunt Marsha, L.J. (Chopper had run away)

One day I had been deer hunting in the woods behind our house, when Larry showed up at the tree stand and ordered me to go home. It was early, and I was confused as he had never done that before. As we headed towards home, I realized he was completely drunk. At 9AM. We entered the house and, as I was

EXTRAORDINARY SOLITUDE

taking off my coveralls, he slapped me hard. He never said a word, no warning at all, just a hard slap right in the face.

I glared at him. "You shouldn't have done that."

We fought like animals right there in the kitchen. Even with my newly honed skills, he eventually overpowered me, immobilizing me in a headlock. Holding me there, he said, "Steven, that's enough. I'm going to let you go. Don't start swinging when I do."

He let me loose, and I glowered at him. Larry never hit me again. But the way he had taught me to fight had truly become a part of me. If anyone ever hit me, I reacted accordingly. That instinctive behavior only got worse as my life continued.

A year or so later, Marsha left Larry for a while, and we drove to California to bring Chopper home. He wasn't the same. He had changed and being with him was different. We had grown apart. Oddly, we never had a physical fight again.

Between the Chapters

While I've written a lot about fighting and violence, my intent isn't to glamorize fighting, sin, or our enemy Satan. Looking back, I know God truly saved my life several times. I could have died in those fights—and both times I fell through the ice. We should give Him a shout of praise for saving us all from death at one time or another.

I'm certain that several demonic spirits had taken up residence in me by the time I turned thirteen. When I was molested, spirits like lust and perversion toward women transferred to me from Damian. Other spirits—hate, rebellion, anger, self-pity, and pride—came along as I experienced physical and emotional abuse. We'll discuss later how to be delivered from demonic spirits. For now, be aware that demons are real and influence a person's personality and thought patterns. Many sicknesses and diseases are demon related.

Christians can open a door and allow foul spirits to demonize them. They cannot be possessed, as the Holy Spirit dwells in us when we give our hearts to Christ, but Christians can certainly be oppressed. I can support this from a Biblical standpoint and from personal experience. The remedy for demons is, and always has been, the name and the blood of Jesus Christ. But both must be applied correctly. We'll discuss this in a later chapter.

For now, I'll tell you about two opposite personalities living in one individual. How can the captain of the chess team be the most prominent drug dealer in a high school of 3,000?

EXTRAORDINARY SOLITUDE

Chapter 4

An Internal Contradiction

"Returning violence for violence multiplies violence, adding deeper darkness to a night already devoid of stars."
(Martin Luther King, Jr.)

Ages 14 to 16

    The type of person I was becoming became even more apparent as I began high school. I possessed a level of determination I haven't found in many others, and I was extraordinarily competitive in all areas of life. A fierce spirit of courage never allowed me to back down or give up. While my IQ was above average, my EQ (emotional intelligence) was below average. Emotional Intelligence enables us to use our emotions to enhance our thoughts and includes our ability to control, express, and evaluate those emotions. In short, I didn't have much of a moral compass. A champion at everything I set my mind to, I was completely dysfunctional at the same time.

I already had an impressive catalog of accomplishments before I turned seventeen. In addition to being a highly sought-after baseball and football champion, I was the Illinois State freshman/sophomore chess champion, a bass tournament winner, the Illinois State under-18 horseshoe pitching champion, and the recipient of MVP awards in many sports. On the flipside, I was selling marijuana and getting high on weed, LSD, and anything else I could get my hands on.

Our baseball league played in a large regional tournament when I was fourteen. We had only won three games the year before, but we had only lost one game so far. We probably would have won that one too if several of our best players hadn't been attending football camp. We won two major tournaments, including the city championship. I played center field in the championship game and batted a thousand. In the semifinals game, I pitched for the win. My performance was covered heavily in the city newspaper in both instances, with photos showing me sliding into bases and hitting a triple.

Was I an all-American boy? Absolutely not. In the one game we lost that season, I was trying to steal third base and would have been out by a mile. Instead of going out gracefully, I slid feet first, ripping the third baseman's arm wide open with my metal cleats. He dropped the ball, and I was declared safe. The damage done to the tendons in his forearm was so significant that he was taken to the hospital by ambulance.

When high school started in the fall, I tried out for the football team. I was an instant success, a star player. Though I was only a freshman, the varsity coach told me to dress for the Friday night football game. Only one other student was given that honor.

During that same week, my girlfriend and I decided to lose our virginities to each other. I was at her house when a friend showed up saying that my brother and his friends were going to the fair and wanted me to go along. I didn't want to go. I wanted to spend the evening as planned. But I allowed myself to be persuaded and left my girlfriend in tears. While at the fair, we came across a pickup football game in one of the fields. My brother convinced me to show off my football skills. The biggest guy on the field was carrying the ball. I ran over and grabbed him, literally ripping the shirt off his body in a solid tackle. End of game.

I walked off the field, eager to check out the rest of the fair with my brother and his friends. We quickly realized we were being followed by a large group of Black guys. Apparently, the man I had tackled was a gang member, a vice lord. His gang brothers demanded that he fight me. My brother, wanting to impress his friends, urged me to accept the challenge.

EXTRAORDINARY SOLITUDE

We found a grassy field towards the back of the fairgrounds.

We both walked to the middle of the circle formed by the spectators, which had grown into an even bigger crowd. My fight training took over, and I crushed my opponent. I got him on the ground in no time and told him to give up. He had no chance, and I was trying to show mercy. He gave up right away, but the other gang members wouldn't accept his defeat. The crowd, in a chaotic frenzy, angrily accused him of not being a real vice lord. Two other vice lords jumped my brother's friend. No one stepped in, so I headed back to help him. A giant blindsided me, punching me in the eye, knocking it loose in its socket.

I'm not sure what my face looked like, but Chopper screamed, "Run!" We took off and made it to a medical tent. I had to see an eye specialist and wore a protective metal patch for a month. The injury ended my football career, and I was never allowed to step into a boxing ring again.

While serving a detention later that fall, I noticed the chess team meeting in a classroom and ducked in to take a peek. The instructor, who didn't know me, told one of the better players to play a game with me. I hadn't played chess in years but managed to play to a stalemate. That schoolteacher/chess instructor became both a mentor and a friend.

I was bored, and my competitive nature took over. Dedicating myself to the chess team, I studied chess and worked at the game by myself for hours. Before long, I was very good. The high school coaches registered us for tournaments throughout the state. At the freshman/sophomore Illinois State Championship tournament, I played board one, where the best player on the team plays. I won the championship. Later that week, an announcement was made over the intercom that Danville High School was home to the new state chess champion. The students were shocked when my name was announced. How could the same kid who sold marijuana and abused alcohol, weed, and LSD be a chess champion?

In the spring of my fifteenth year, Uncle Larry was in a period of sobriety and had become the president of the local Bass Club. In the first tournament of the year, club participants were allowed to bring their own partner. Larry selected me as his partner thinking he would keep all the prize money if we won. I caught five keeper largemouth bass, while the entire field of competitors only caught seven total! We won by a large margin. I had never seen Larry so happy and proud of me. The tournament was a highlight in our relationship.

I met Barbie during that same summer. She became my girlfriend and, eventually, the mother of my two daughters. Barbie lived with her grandparents. Her grandfather was a competitive horseshoe pitcher who introduced me to the sport. In the evenings, we pitched horseshoes in his backyard.

EXTRAORDINARY SOLITUDE

After my skill improved to the point where I could be competitive, he took me with him to tournaments in Illinois and Indiana. I won the State of Illinois horseshoe championship in the under-18 division.

Even with noteworthy accomplishments to be proud of, I still couldn't claim the title of all-American boy. I obviously had intellect and a keen competitive nature that pushed me to excel when I wanted. But there was a dark side always pulling me towards the shadows. One time, as I stood by the side of the road with my bicycle, an older teenager drove by with his girlfriend. He made a few smart comments to show off, then jumped out of his car intent on putting his hands on me. He had no idea that I was capable of beating him so badly. I ripped off his earrings and sent him back to his girlfriend, humiliated and in pain.

During the same time period, Barbie found me in a pool hall and told me her grandfather had been bullied by hoodlums while riding his bike. I left with her, intent on getting the details directly from him. We arrived back in the neighborhood to find all the old men standing in the street. Barbie's grandfather said a group of thugs had approached him while he was riding around the block. He handed me a 3-wood golf club and pointed in the direction the gang had taken. I took off with another kid as my companion. We found the hoods—around a dozen of them—in a park. The odds were pretty good. Them against me, a three wood, and a kid. I asked which one had threatened the old man on a bike. The ringleader stepped forward, and I smacked him in the forehead with the golf club. Adrenalin had already kicked in, and I would have hit him again . . . and again . . . and again, probably killing him or, at the least, severely injuring him. And then God moved. Of course, I didn't recognize His hand at the time, but I can now identify a miracle when I see one.

A massive fog fell over the entire park, dropping like a blanket in an absolute millisecond! The entire world disappeared in the blink of an eye. I couldn't see five inches in front of my face. Neither could anyone else. The thugs scattered and ran. I couldn't see my friend. I couldn't find the bullies or the guy I had bashed with the golf club. When the fog lifted about ten minutes later, I stood alone in the park. I found my friend later, but neither of us could explain what had happened.

Even though I was only fifteen, Barbie and I moved in with Chopper and his girlfriend, Melony. Now that I was responsible for paying bills and taking care of Barbie, Chopper, and Melony, I took the weed business more seriously and began selling marijuana full time. We had been poor my entire life, and I was tired of it and of everything that came along with being poor. I woke up every morning and got high. Some days I went to school; some days I didn't. The days fell into a pattern: have sex, get high, sell weed, get drunk. Do it all again the next day.

EXTRAORDINARY SOLITUDE

And then I decided it wasn't enough. I wanted more—needed more. I would put my efforts into expanding. I would become the most successful drug trafficker in the Midwest.

Chapter 5

The Deepening Darkness

*"There is no neutral ground in the universe.
Every square inch, every split second
is claimed by God, and counterclaimed by Satan."*
(C. S. Lewis)

Ages 17 to 19

I sold most of my weed to the Black crack dealers at school. Straight out of the projects, they recognized the fact that I saw no skin color. I skipped school regularly to smoke blunts with my Black friends. I also obtained large quantities of weed from the Mexicans. My partners in crime were of all ethnicities, and race wasn't an issue. They also respected me because I didn't pretend to be Black. I wasn't raised in the hood. I was poor, white, and got along with Blacks and Spanish equally.

After making a solid Mexican connection, I turned Chopper's house into a non-stop, 24-hour weed business, and the money rolled in. I took great pleasure in showing off to my nerdy friends at chess tournaments by flashing $3,000 or $4,000 in $20 bills. Even though they were from rich families, they had never seen so much cash. I did my best to hook up these future doctors, lawyers, and scientists with call girls while staying in hotels at out-of-town chess tournaments.

It wasn't long before my drinking rose another level. Due to no fault of her own, my feelings for Barbie waned, and I cheated on her repeatedly. Women threw themselves at me. I was turning into a lunatic, edging further toward the edge, sleeping with several women a day, and knocking out grown men in bars. Nothing in life made sense.

One night, while tripping on LCD, Chopper, his friend Andy, and I decided to drive to Florida—another example of our spur-of-the-moment craziness. We stopped in Arkansas on our way back to meet some of Andy's family. They had good homes but were all strung out on methamphetamines. During the trip, I was robbed while conducting a huge drug deal. At this point, I had quit school and was a full-on drug addict. I owed money to drug dealers, but I was broke after the robbery. As the threads unraveled, God showed up again. This time He used a person.

One day, while at Chopper's house, Bill, my chess coach, called. He wanted to know why I had dropped out of school and what was going on in my

EXTRAORDINARY SOLITUDE

life. I told him he really didn't want to know. Convincing me of his interest, he took me to Arby's where I unloaded the events of the last couple of years. I knew he would be shocked, and he was. Then he looked me right in the eye, telling me I could leave that environment right then and there and live with him and his wife.

There were conditions. I had to make the move immediately and go back to school. I agreed. Gathering my clothes and meager belongings at Chopper's, I left, much to the shock and chagrin of my brother, his girlfriend, and Barbie.

Bill and his wife, Jane, lived in a large house in a good neighborhood. Wanting to fit in, I changed the way I dressed and the way I studied in school. I tried to change my friends. Sober and exposed to a different way of living, my life was the best it had ever been. These good people treated me like family.

With their support, I graduated by going to high school full time and attending alternative school as well. Immediately enrolling in the local junior college for the summer semester, I was high on life. But I made a foolish error in judgment. I started hanging out with new friends who wanted to drink and do cocaine. I could always get drugs, so they never failed to include me when they got together. Drugs and alcohol were recreational fun for them, but restarted an old cycle for me.

EXTRAORDINARY SOLITUDE

As I visited some of my old drug buddies, a dealer walked through the front room and into a back bedroom with one of my friends. They were doing a drug deal. Afterwards, I asked what the deal was about and was told that they had to pay extremely high prices to survive after I left the business. Without me, they no longer had a close, reliable connection. I made a couple of phone calls and, just like that, I was back in the drug business.

A few weeks later, it dawned on me that I had a large amount of marijuana in Bill and Jane's basement. I couldn't put these good people in jeopardy, so I moved out, breaking their hearts. But I couldn't do drugs and deal drugs under their roof, and I was already back in the lifestyle.

There's no need to describe what I went through after leaving Bill and Jane's home. Drug dealers, as well as the media and music industry, often glamorize the lifestyle. Most people I met and dealt with were absolutely miserable and spent every moment looking over their shoulders in panicked paranoia. Their lives were continually in danger from both cops and robbers. I, too, was a miserable person the entire time I sold and used drugs. I hated myself and punished myself. Satan, the enemy, was trying to kill me, and I was helping him. I couldn't stop the cycle. My determination to break free was hindered by the fact that I hated poverty more than I hated the drug life.

EXTRAORDINARY SOLITUDE

The pain of abuse had to be numbed somehow. If I was going to be a drug dealer, I would be a big one. The possibility of dying in prison didn't scare me. All forms of wickedness thrive in an environment such as the one I created for myself. Hell-bent on destroying myself, memories from that time come in bits and pieces, one long blur of women, drugs, and money.

To move up the ladder to the source of the drugs, I had to get closer to Mexico. A flight from Indianapolis, Indiana, to McAllen, Texas, permitted me to hook up with my Mexican connection on his home turf. Once in McAllen, my connection got drunk and passed out, so I bypassed him and used *his* connection. Traveling to Texas on a regular basis, I paid Bobby, a friend, to fly with me. We eventually got caught with twenty pounds of marijuana. An investigation tracked another twenty pounds of weed I had sent to Illinois.

Bobby and Steven before their arrest

EXTRAORDINARY SOLITUDE

The jail on the Mexican border was filthy and overcrowded, and no one spoke much if any English. We were teenagers in a strange and dark place. After the second day with no phone call, Bobby could no longer control his emotions. He was scared and broke into tears. I crossed the cell and, in the loudest voice I could muster, sang *Oye Como Va*, the only Spanish song I knew. The Mexicans loved it and gathered at the bars of their cells, yelling and singing along. I had accomplished my goal, breaking the tension and affording Bobby some protection. The humor of the whole situation lifted Bobby's spirits and helped calm him down.

A couple of days later, we went to court and were transferred to a larger, more modern jail. Because I couldn't give an address for a mother or father, my bond was set higher than Bobby's. I bonded him out first, as he was having such a hard time, and he was released.

I was taken to a cell block upstairs where I realized, once again, that I was the only white man behind bars. Everyone else was part of a Spanish gang. After putting the mattress together, I climbed onto my bed.

"I like your shoes," said the Mexican on the bunk below me.

"So do I," I responded.

"No. I want them. Give them to me."

EXTRAORDINARY SOLITUDE

I wasn't about to give him my shoes—or anything else. If I didn't stand tough from the beginning, I would be seen as weak. I had to be smart . . . and strong.

"Let me get down, and I'll let you have them."

When my feet hit the floor, I moved to a better position in the middle of the day room and took up a boxing stance.

Immediately, the Mexicans came together, moving in like a wave. A spokesman emerged from the mob.

"Jorje is receiving a life sentence," he said in broken English. "He may never have a new pair of shoes again."

My thoughts whirled. I could win the fight . . . and keep my shoes. But who knew how many others I would have to fight? Did I really want to get into it with my Mexican cellmate in a jail filled with Mexican thugs? I tried another tactic. "I'll make you a deal, I'm keeping my shoes—for now. But I'll give them to him when I make bond. You have my word."

A glance passed between them, and they agreed.

Unbelievable! God intervened on my behalf again, though I wouldn't give Him the credit for many years.

A day or two later, I made bond. I walked out of the cell block and down the hall. Then I stopped and told the officer I had to go back. He gave me the oddest look. Was I crazy? I insisted, and he let me walk back to the bars.

"Jorje! Come here!" I yelled.

He approached hesitantly as if unsure what I would do. Spit on him? Throw a punch?

"Do you still want my shoes?"

A look of surprise flitted across his face. "Sí. I do."

I took off my shoes and handed them to him through the bars. I had kept my word, and a lifer had a new pair of shoes.

Bobby and I reconnected after I was released, staying in south Texas at the home of a corrupt cop. Returning to Illinois was out of the question, as I was wanted for the weed I had transported earlier. High on coke, we hung out until we could catch a Greyhound bus to Bobby's father's place in Florida. When we arrived, Bobby's father refused to let me stay. Where was I supposed to go? All my money was in Illinois. I flew to Virginia and went to see Nancy, my biological mother. I got a plane ticket for Barbie, and she joined us.

Ironically, my mother was a fairly big weed dealer herself. I went to work trying to get my sources to send marijuana for her to sell. Before long, Mom went on a major crack binge and disappeared for days, something her husband, Joe, said she did occasionally. When she returned several days later, she and Joe had a fist fight. Mom pulled out a pistol and put the barrel in her mouth. I begged her to not pull the trigger, and she relented. Death was averted, at least that day.

Later, when Mom was out of the house, I told Barbie we were leaving. I picked Mom's safe with a screwdriver and took about $10,000 in cash and around a pound of weed. Barbie and I hopped a Greyhound and headed south.

Deciding to head back to Illinois, we got off the bus in Savannah, Georgia. I bought a used car, paying with cash and a portion of the marijuana. When we reached Ohio, I stopped to visit a friend and made the mistake of telling him I was on the run. He told his wife, and his wife called the police. I was arrested and taken to the police station. A detective informed me there was an outstanding warrant for me in Virginia. Mom had reported the theft. I processed the information and worked up a couple of tears, twisting the truth and saying the inmates in Texas had stolen my shoes. I acted as pathetic as I could, saying I was afraid of the same thing happening again and begged him to let me give the shoes I was wearing to Barbie for safekeeping. He said I could, and Barbie went back to Illinois with the $5,000 I had hidden under the insoles.

Two weeks later, I was flown back to the old, dank jail in Hampton, Virginia. Most of the other prisoners were African-Americans. A giant Black man named Dewayne beat me out of $10 playing 3-card

EXTRAORDINARY SOLITUDE

Monte. He hustled me, and I respected the hustle. We agreed I would pay him when we went to the commissary, but he was transferred to another jail. On commissary day, a friend of his came by my cell for the $10. I refused, saying I would only give the money to Dewayne.

A couple of weeks later, Dewayne returned to the cell block. He didn't stop to see me but went straight to his friend for his money. A few minutes later, he walked into my cell and asked why I hadn't handed over the money. I repeated what I had said before—I would only pay the person I owed. He slapped me in the face, a terrible mistake on his part. I jumped up and beat him across the day room, as the other inmates watched in shock.

The guards didn't see what was going on—or they pretended not to—as blood spattered the walls. When it was obvious Dewayne was no longer a threat, I lowered my fists. Severely injured, he was transported to a local hospital.

After I bonded out of the jail in Virginia a few months later, I made my way back to Illinois to retrieve the money owed to me. Somehow the cops were tipped off and stopped my car. I was arrested again and taken to jail in Illinois for the twenty pounds of marijuana the police had found when I was in Texas. I sold my car and bonded out of the Illinois jail. I was out of jail but had no money and no car.

EXTRAORDINARY SOLITUDE

I moved in with Aunt Marsha again. Before long I met Susie, one of my brother's friends. Barbie and I were no longer together, and Susie and I hit it off right away. She liked bad boys, and I certainly qualified. Susie was beautiful, smart, and funny, and about four years younger than I. When I could scrape together a couple hundred dollars, we would rent a hotel room and go to dinner or play pool. I wasn't easy to love, and she begged me to stop drinking and using drugs. I couldn't stop even though I loved her. I was facing cases in multiple states and convinced myself I needed the drugs and alcohol to escape the reality I had created.

On Christmas morning, Larry and I drove to my grandmother's house for dinner. I told Larry I was going to kill Damian, who had molested me as a child. The plan was simple: walk in the house and blow his head off right there in the front room. Larry somehow talked me out of it, saving Damian from dying by my hand that day. Damian will never understand that it was only by God's hand through Larry that he wasn't murdered that Christmas. I was out of control and would have easily shot Damian and then sat down to a turkey dinner. This is another incident where I look back and say, "Thank You, Jesus, for having mercy on me that day."

Chopper and I were surprised when Larry, on a day he was sober, asked us to help him pick up an air-conditioning unit in Indiana. The request was odd because we never did anything together anymore. As Larry drove us home, he announced he wanted to pray. What? Larry wanted to pray? In all the years we had spent together, I had never heard him pray even once. He prayed with strength and energy, asking for God's protection over us. I smirked as he prayed and admit to being a bit unnerved when he said, "Steven, you think that prayer was for Chopper, but it was for you. I think something bad is about to happen." The prayer came out of nowhere from the mouth of a man I couldn't have imagined praying. Somehow, the Lord had put it on Larry's heart to pray for me.

A few months later, as I lay in bed, miserable with a hangover and a stuffed-up nose after a night of filling it with cocaine, the phone rang. I almost fell on the floor when I heard Jane's voice on the other end of the line, asking if I had a winter coat. I didn't. Bill had bought a new leather jacket and wanted me to have his old one. I drove over to get it, and we spent a couple of hours catching up. I left with the jacket and checked myself into rehab. Having limited space, the rehab facility allowed me to stay only a couple of days. Bill and Jane picked me up when I was discharged and asked if I wanted to live with them again.

Bill and Jane allowing me to come back into their home, into their lives, was probably the greatest act of human kindness I had ever experienced. They wanted nothing from me but that I would have a good life. For me to have more than a fair chance. I will always be thankful for them. Unfortunately, none of us had any way of knowing how bound I was by the enemy. What drove me? Did I just need to sober up? Would counseling do the trick? We didn't know, and they tried everything. They loved me like one of their own children.

What an incredible opportunity—a lifeline. But could I hold on to it?

EXTRAORDINARY SOLITUDE

Chapter 6

Hitting Bottom

"The devil knows if he can capture your thought life he has won a mighty victory over you."
(Smith Wigglesworth)

Ages 20 to 24

Moving in with Bill and Jane again was the lifeline I so desperately needed. I took the opportunity seriously and was determined to comply to their new rules. Things would be different this time.

Uncle Larry, in his early forties, died soon after. Though urged by his doctors to quit drinking, he couldn't stop and had destroyed his liver. Larry asked L.J. to climb into bed with him. After reading the Bible out loud for a while, he told L.J., who was around ten, to call an ambulance. He died at the hospital.

Larry's death hurt me badly. Despite his abuse and drunken behavior, I loved him and cried like a baby at his funeral.

EXTRAORDINARY SOLITUDE

Barbie and I had been unaware she was pregnant when I left her to be with Susie. Around the same time as Larry's passing, Barbie gave birth to our daughter, Katie. We were all in love the moment we laid eyes on her. Jane insisted I go to court, set up visitation rights, and pay child support. I was still with Susie, but Bill and Jane didn't support our relationship. They sensed trouble, and Bill advised me on multiple occasions to stay away from her. He insisted I was too mature at 21 to be with a 17-year-old. I wasn't using or drinking and was convinced I loved her.

I needed employment most of all and began selling cars at a dealership. Working a job was new, but dressing nice and being sober felt fantastic. Then I met another girl. Gorgeous and of Indian descent, Sarah had a daughter just a little bit older than Katie. I dropped Susie without blinking. Bill and Jane liked Sarah, and everything was going well in my life. I spent a lot of time with my daughter and considered settling down with Sarah.

I still had to contend with legal issues. Bill and Jane found a fantastic lawyer, and I was relieved to get probation in Illinois and Virginia. The prosecutor in Texas dropped all charges as I had pled guilty in two other states. Finally, life was turning around for me. And it happened quickly within about eight or nine months.

Then the wheels fell off again. I started hanging out with friends from work, partying and drinking at the clubs on weekends. I cheated on Sarah with Susie. I can't explain my backslide. I just lost my mind again. I didn't think of myself as a bad person, but old thoughts and patterns followed alcohol and drugs. When I saw an old drug connection at work, I jumped right back into the cocaine business. Did I love my daughter? Did I love Bill and Jane? Yes, and yes. Did I love myself? Not even close. I hated myself. My life fell apart so fast there was no way I could hold on. I broke up with Sarah and went back to Susie. Then I moved out of Bill and Jane's house . . . again.

When I drank, I drank until I passed out. When I got high, I would keep going until I couldn't breathe. Every single time. I went back. Back to drugs. Back to alcohol. Back to death's doorstep. Back to hell. I quit my job and went back full time to baggies and scales. My reputation as a drug trafficker grew as I became more and more successful.

Susie hated my lifestyle. She begged me to stop drinking. She pleaded with me to stop selling drugs. I couldn't do either. I would take a day off from getting high or drunk, but I would go even harder the next day. I knew nothing but misery but couldn't seem to make a change that lasted. The downward spiral seemed to have no end.

During the summer of 1998, Chopper and I, along with Susie and a friend of hers, were at my apartment watching the Bulls play the Utah Jazz. Susie and I began to argue, and she threw a glass at me. I grabbed her by the arm, shoved her out of the house, and locked the door. Nothing more physical than that took place, but she called the cops, and I spent the night in jail. When I came home the next day, I found Susie sitting in the front room. We made up in the usual way, and everything went back to normal.

A week or two later, I forced Susie out of my house again. I left as well, but she had called the police, and they pulled me over a short time later. Even though I had not hit her either time, the incidents were considered domestic abuse. The real issue for me was that I was still on probation in two states. These false domestic battery charges could put me in violation of either probation and land me in jail for many years. So, when I got out this time, I called a few friends and borrowed a pickup truck. We went to my house to get my furniture and personal property. When I unlocked the door, Susie was sitting in the front room, obviously expecting things to go back to normal. They were not. I wouldn't fall for her game this time. My friends and I loaded up everything I owned and left Susie standing in an empty apartment. After I left, I made my way to Barbie's place and stayed with her for a couple of weeks. I'm ashamed to admit I used Barbie, like I used so many others during those years.

Meanwhile, Susie and I started talking over the phone, trying to repair our relationship and work things out. We agreed to meet in a Hardee's parking

EXTRAORDINARY SOLITUDE

lot. I followed her home to drop off her car, then drove my car to a liquor store. We headed for one of our old parking spots where we used to have sex before we got an apartment. We drank throughout the evening and had makeup sex like lovers do. But then everything hidden came to the surface and an argument ensued. I had been living with Barbie, and Susie was livid. The fight escalated and Susie slapped me in the face. We were now in a full-fledged domestic dispute. Once we calmed down, she asked me to take her to the hospital. I must have been too drunk to understand her motives, because I innocently did as she asked. Within twelve hours, the police picked me up, and I went to jail and was booked. I couldn't believe the charges, carrying decades of prison time, that were being laid against me.

Twenty-six years later, it's still hard to believe how everything went south so badly and how lost I was. God is so merciful. His nature is to be loving and full of mercy and grace. At this moment, when I was such a wretched sinner, God saved my life again. He reached down and protected me in my darkest hour. Even though I had opened the door for the enemy to come in, God was still my shield.

I was housed on the top floor of the county jail with a population that was predominantly African-American. The recreation yard, nothing more than a large concrete slab with bricks on all sides and a fence over an open roof, boasted a makeshift volleyball net made from cut sheets. A game was in process, a sock stuffed with toilet paper serving as the ball. I joined in, playing barefoot on the concrete slab because we weren't allowed to wear shoes. During one of the games, I jumped up and spiked the ball, accidentally hitting a giant, muscle-bound Black man in the face. I asked him if he was cool, and he said he was. I turned to walk back to the service area and took my eyes off him for just a moment. He came up from behind and—BAM!—hit me in the side of the face, his fist like a sledgehammer. Stunned and wobbling, my head on fire, it's a wonder I wasn't knocked completely out.

    My jaw was broken in two spots, on the side, which is most common, but also straight down the middle at my chin so that my bottom teeth separated. The giant continued to pummel me. By the grace of God, I remained on my feet—dazed and hurt but standing. He threw his weight into every punch, doing his best to knock me out. My training instincts finally kicked in, and I began ducking, dodging, and blocking. Once I got my bearings back, I hit him with everything I had left, throwing combinations and punches from every angle. This guy was huge. If I hit the ground, he could easily kill me.

    One of my overhand rights finally got through and slammed into his chin. Now *he* was backpedaling, on the defensive. Everyone watched in shock. My opponent had been in jail for five years awaiting a murder trial. A callous bully, the list of inmates he had beaten up was long. I managed to back him up against the wall. I couldn't gather the strength to finish him off, because I couldn't breathe. My nose was shattered, broken in more places than the doctor could count, and my mouth was filled with blood. We both stopped fighting and stared at each other. It was over. I had survived.

My jaw was wired shut and a large tube placed in my nose so I could breathe. Adding to these injuries, the soles of my feet were raw. I had scraped off all the skin fighting barefoot on concrete. I was in the hospital for three days and in solitary confinement for six weeks. I have no doubt that this was another time God saved my life. Had I been knocked out or taken to the floor, that man would have killed me or, at the least, left me brain damaged.

Eighty-six days after entering county jail, I went to court and took an Alford plea, which means I believed the court had enough evidence to find me guilty, but I was admitting absolutely no guilt. The prosecutor doesn't have to accept an Alford plea, neither does the sentencing judge. Several of Susie's claims weren't true, and I think the judge and the prosecutor realized parts of her story made no sense. Even so, I would have been found guilty had we gone to trial.

The main evidence against me was age. I was a 21-year-old who was living with and having sex with a 17-year-old. The Alford plea was accepted, and I was sentenced to four-and-a-half years in the penitentiary. I would most likely serve about half that time.

When the prison doors slammed shut behind me, my anger and hate converged into full-blown craziness, and I tattooed "INSANE" on my chest under a giant Cobra face. I hooked up with gang members in the penitentiary and volunteered to do a hit during my first year. Someone had already been assigned the job, but I was ready to go. That's how insane I was at the time. I didn't kill the guy, but I forced him and his crew to leave the prison, which gained me major status.

I'm only going to make three main points about this three-year stint in prison. Number one: I did not seek God. Number two: I still did drugs. Number three: I had no plan for when I got out. When I was released from Statesville Penitentiary in Illinois, detectives picked me up for violating my probation in Virginia. While I was housed in Virginia awaiting my day in court, a man in my unit told me he knew who I was. There was no way he knew me, as I had just finished three years in an Illinois state penitentiary. His name was Moon Dog, and he insisted he knew exactly who I was. I couldn't have been more surprised when he said he knew my mother. They had been childhood friends and had run in the same circles their whole lives.

EXTRAORDINARY SOLITUDE

According to Moon Dog, my mom had something important to tell me. I called and asked her to visit me. We sat across from each other, and she said that the courts had granted her custody again when I was about five years old. Moon Dog had paid for her trip to Illinois so she could retrieve Chopper and me. But we had forgotten her, and she didn't have the heart to take us away from the only home we knew. She confirmed that Chopper and I had different fathers and, for the first time, told me my biological father's name. She told me she had forgiven me for stealing her money and marijuana when I went on the run.

In prison at 23

After my court hearing, she and I spent a couple of days getting drunk together. She told me amazing stories from the time I was born until she lost me to foster care. One, time, when I was less than two years old, I straddled a windowsill with one leg in the house and the other hanging out of the window. A man, who had gotten into an argument with one of my uncles, showed up in our yard carrying a machete. He strode up to the window and reached for my leg, intending to hack it off. My grandmother came out of the house with a shotgun and started shooting.

Mom told me how hard her life had been. She had been in many abusive relationships and had been beaten innumerable times. A self-made woman, she had educated herself and worked as a tax consultant, filing taxes for clients by computer. She also ran a small, sophisticated, marijuana business. I was impressed.

Chopper in Myrtle Beach, SC, on his way to visit Steven in Butner, NC

EXTRAORDINARY SOLITUDE

My probation in Virginia had been extended and would run concurrently with my Illinois parole, so I had to leave Virginia after a few days to report for parole in Illinois. I would never see my mother again. She committed suicide in 2003. I didn't learn the details of her death until Chopper visited me several years later. He had been with her when she jumped out of a vehicle going 65 mph.

I knew I was on that same highway—the road of destruction... and death.

EXTRAORDINARY SOLITUDE

Part Two
Reborn

EXTRAORDINARY SOLITUDE

Chapter 7

Lost and Found

*"There is no pit so deep that
God's love is not deeper still."*
(Corrie ten Boom)

Age 25

I reported for parole in Illinois and was fitted with an ankle monitor I had to wear for two years. Aunt Marsha's house was listed as my release address. She had a new husband, Jim, who was an alcoholic. He woke up at 6AM and would drink until he went to bed at 10PM. The only saving grace was that he wasn't a violent drunk, and Marsha seemed to be happy.

Barbie showed up on Marsha's doorstep one day and convinced me to live with her again. I agreed and, after a month trying to find a job, I decided to get back into the drug business. Connections were established with just a few phone calls, and I started selling cocaine full time. Barbie would have none of it. She packed up and left.

Before long, I found a new girlfriend—the sister of a good friend—and we moved in together. Jessica was my good friend's sister. We had grown up together, and, knowing how I had been raised, she thought she understood my craziness.

I worked my way up the drug ladder from one kilo, to two kilos, and upwards. Recruiting guys I'd known since childhood, I flooded the community with cocaine. My movements were hampered by the ankle monitor, so I made up a "legitimate" business. I bought a lot of tools, opened a woodshop, and hired other dealers in my organization. We hung around the woodshop, getting drunk and high all day. I would call my parole officer and say I needed to work until 2 or 3 in the morning, and I would be granted permission to move around during that time. On any given day I could make $5,000 to $10,000 profit selling cocaine. I was still a miserable, miserable man, getting high to the point of nearly overdosing. Barbie had recently given birth to my daughter, Jenna, and Jessica was seven months pregnant with my son. The demons were taking over again. It was time for another crash.

Out at a club one night, while I was drunk on whiskey and high on pills, my friend, Bobby, told me he was having trouble with someone. I told him to signal who the guy was by putting his arm around him. Bobby walked off, and I continued to drink. Another

EXTRAORDINARY SOLITUDE

man joined me at the bar and asked if I remembered him. When I said I didn't, he turned, exposing a nasty scar on his face. The skin and meat had been removed from the high point of his cheek. I remembered him instantly. I had done that to him. He met my gaze and told me it was all good—and bought me another drink.

I had fought him in a boat lot when I was 17 years old. I had given his girlfriend a ride. I never kissed her or laid a hand on her, but he was mad and took a swing at me. Slipping on the rocks, I slammed my head on a concrete parking block. Blood gushed down my face and into my eyes from the gash in my forehead. He fell on me, but when he lifted off to punch me, I grabbed his head and pulled it down, biting off a huge chunk of his face. He screamed and pulled away. Once I got to my feet, the fight was over for him. I used my boxing skills to destroy him. His friends tried to stop the fight, and I punched them, too. Later, when I was at the hospital waiting for stitches, he came in the lobby, and I jumped on him again. The police separated us, and we both got the medical treatment we needed.

Now, nearly nine years later, I was drinking whiskey with him in a bar. He wanted to shake hands, and I was willing. Throwing back a shot, I spied Bobby with his arm around the guy he claimed had given him trouble. I told the scarred man that he was about to see something spectacular. He mouthed, "Oh no," as I jumped off the barstool and headed for the pool table.

EXTRAORDINARY SOLITUDE

Grabbing a pool ball, I smacked Bobby's nemesis in the head. All hell broke loose, and, before I knew it, a group of guys came to his defense, and I found myself on the floor. The man I had hit was one of the bouncers.

Bobby yelled that he had a gun, even though he didn't. We ran out the door and jumped in my car. As soon as I put the key in the ignition, the police had a pistol pointed at my head. I went back to prison for 90 days for violating my parole, missing the birth of my son, Steven.

Even in prison, I kept things moving. I had buried more than two kilos in the woods behind my house. A friend visited me, and I told him the location of the drugs. He dug them up and continued to sell for me while I sat in prison. When my three-month sentence was served and I was released, I picked up where I had left off and continued my destructive path for the next seven months. I cleared $60,000 in profits the last month I was a free man. Sleeping with Jessica's friend on the side, strung out on drugs, I was out of control and dangerous.

To make matters even worse, I began binging on meth, staying awake for five days at a time, and suffering from hallucinations. During one of these binges, I was hell-bent on self-destruction and so under the influence of demonic forces that I heated up a knife with a propane torch and pressed it to my chest trying to remove the word "insane." I applied the blazing, orange-hot knife multiple times to remove the tattoo completely. The burn got infected, but I refused to go to the doctor at first. I finally sought treatment and had the infection cut out when Jessica couldn't stand the smell anymore.

At the beach with his stepson, Kaleb, a month before Steven's arrest

    One of my dealers had made an agreement with the feds. He had cocaine in his possession that belonged to me, so a plan was concocted to entrap me. Unfortunately, the plan didn't go exactly as hoped. His wife called my house to tell me to come get the cocaine. I had just come off a recent meth binge and was finally resting, so I had Jessica take the call. The drugs needed to be picked up, but Jessica didn't want me to leave the house, fearing I wouldn't come back for days. If she didn't want me to leave, she would have to pick up the drugs for me. So she did . . . and was arrested.

EXTRAORDINARY SOLITUDE

After grabbing Jessica, the DEA and FBI raided our house and found six kilos in my business trailer. A couple hundred thousand dollars was owed to me on the streets. Of course, I lost everything. But I wasn't the only one who lost. Innocent people always get caught up in the wake of destruction. And Jessica was caught.

One of the first things the DEA asks is if you're willing to cooperate and turn in other drug dealers in exchange for a reduced sentence. I made a deal to cooperate with the DEA *if* they would release Jessica. They agreed. As soon as she was released, I spread the word to my childhood friends, letting them know that I had been busted by the DEA. I warned them not to answer the phone if I called and not to answer their doors if I showed up at their houses. As a result, only two people went to prison—Jessica and me.

I had made things worse for us both. The DEA was outraged that I had broken our agreement and had, instead, warned everyone. They put me in jail, but were still interested in taking down some dirty cops. I didn't mind giving up dirty cops, but the feds were so angry with me that they sent in their B-Team, state internal affairs, instead of the FBI to investigate. In the end, they weren't really interested in the cops, just in drug dealers. It was all smoke and mirrors. The specifics were revealed later in federal court. My case was included in a book titled, *Too Politically*

EXTRAORDINARY SOLITUDE

Sensitive, by Michael Callahan in the chapter "Conspiracy at the Top."

The enemy had such a strong grip on my life. Even though I was facing decades in prison, I wasn't willing to yield to God on any level. I had no desire to change my thought patterns, no desire to get clean and sober, no desire to make a better life for myself.

While in federal custody, I still tried collecting money owed me so I could provide for Jessica and our children. Being a well-known drug dealer and renowned street fighter made me a powerful influence in our community. It made perfect sense to me to have L.J., my little brother, collect the money on my behalf. When he visited me in jail, I told him where to go and how to go about the job. I gave him a sign with a finger and a thumb. He knew what that sign meant.

After about a week, I called home. To this day I can't remember who I spoke to, but the conversation went something like this:

"Steven, have you been watching the news the past couple of days?"

I hadn't.

"Okay listen, everything is going to be all right. L.J. was in a terrible car wreck. He shot up some drug dealer's houses and got into a high-speed chase with the cops. He's in bad shape and is on a life-support breathing machine."

That was all I heard. Stunned and numb, I hung up the phone. Once I was back in my cell, I fell to my knees, devastated, my heart ripped in two. There was no way to escape the truth: I had destroyed another loved one.

Nicknames were common on the street, and I had been called by different names, like Rooster and Red. But one guy used to call me "The Devil." Finally broken by what had happened to L.J., I wondered if I truly might be the devil? I cried out to Jesus on that jail floor, confessing I couldn't take any more. Surrendering my life to Him right there and then, I tried to make a deal. The rest of my life would be His, if He saved L.J. Admittedly, I didn't feel any different afterwards, as all my thoughts were focused on L.J., but a simple prayer from the heart is all that's needed. God was in control, and I had given Him the right-of-way in my life.

I got updates on L.J. during the next couple of weeks. Jessica's aunt, who was a pastor, visited L.J. in the hospital. She laid hands on him and declared he would not die but live. I didn't start reading the Bible right away or join a prayer group. In fact, not much changed at all. Then God moved. The feds transferred me to another holding jail, and life returned to normalcy. Sadly, I didn't give God a second thought. Word came that L.J. would live, but with slight brain damage and metal plates all over his body. He had to learn to walk, read, and write all over again.

Then it happened. Out of nowhere, the whisper of the Holy Spirit told me I shouldn't eat but should read the Bible instead. I now know this is called fasting, but I didn't know it then. Unable to shake the conviction, I borrowed a King James Bible from an old Black man in my cell block. Bible in hand, I stayed in my cell. I didn't eat anything that day but, instead, read the Bible. I continued reading until I completed the entire Bible. It took 11 days. When I returned the book to the old man, I told him about the revelation I had received and added, "Pop, this is the greatest love letter ever written." He said I could borrow it anytime, and I often took advantage of his offer. From that moment, God was on me and His presence was all around me!

    The cell block was small with only about 10 beds. I was the only white guy there, but everyone was cool. The TV continuously broadcast BET, while I stayed in my cell reading and rereading the Bible. One day, the old man switched the TV to a Christian program and asked if I wanted to watch it with him. Absolutely! I had very little exposure to the Bible or its teachings in my life and was eager to learn more and more.

    Gang members soon starting watching the programs with me. Then we started praying and reading the Word in my cell. Scriptures leaped off the pages of the Bible, and I wrote them on the wall in pencil. Before long, my cell was entirely covered with the Word of God. My family thought I had lost my mind when I told them I had found Jesus. Considering all the terrible things I'd done in my life, I thought it was funny that *now* they thought I was crazy. But I had God and I knew it. He had been with me my whole life, but I had never seen Him. I had been blinded by the enemy.

My sentencing date drew near, and I anticipated that I could get no less than 262 months in federal prison. I would have to serve about 87-percent of that time, around 230 months. I had just turned 26 years old when I caught the case with the DEA, so I would be around 45 when released. My lawyer and I felt confident Jessica would get probation. Unfortunately, the sentencing guidelines were mandatory, and she had to serve a minimum of 24 months. She was only 22 years old.

I cried at sentencing for two reasons. First, Jessica was going to prison, and our kids would be without both parents. Second, because I was a broken man, and I had caused a tremendous amount of death and destruction in my life and in the lives of those around me.

I explained the circumstances of the case to the sentencing judge and begged him to give me any time he was mandated to give Jessica. She didn't deserve to serve time. She wasn't a drug dealer but had been caught in a circumstance that was of my doing. Unfortunately, he couldn't do anything and said the DEA and FBI knew what they were doing when they pressed charges against Jessica. They also knew the judge's hands would be tied regarding sentencing.

The prosecutor requested I be sentenced to 288 months, as I had played games with the DEA and warned potential drug targets to shut down their operations. The judge didn't buy it, saying 262 months was enough. Jessica eventually received a year off her two-year sentence by completing a drug program in prison. She would be out in less than 12 months.

Jessica with Kaleb on visitation day in Federal prison

I remained in jail until the US Marshals arrived to fly me to the Federal Prison Complex in Coleman, Florida. Coleman has five federal prisons in the complex, and I was housed in the medium-high-security facility. I knew I wasn't alone; the Lord had promised to be with me wherever I went. Serving out

EXTRAORDINARY SOLITUDE

my sentence would be far different than before. I would serve out my time, not as a violent gang banger, but as a servant of the Most High God.

Between the Chapters

If you aren't saved, it's important that you know Jesus isn't hiding from you. The enemy and his demons have worked hard to blind your mind and your heart. Keep reading. In a later chapter, I'll tell you how to get the blinders off and let the light in.

Second Corinthians 4:3-4 tells us,

"But even if our gospel is veiled, it is veiled to those who are perishing, whose minds the god of this age has blinded, who do not believe, lest the light of the gospel of the glory of Christ, who is the image of God, should shine on them."

EXTRAORDINARY SOLITUDE

Chapter 8

Two Steps Forward ...
One Step Back

*"Beware of no man more than of yourself;
we carry our worst enemies within us."*
(Charles Spurgeon)

Age 26

Some of the most religious groups in prisons are basically just gangs. Christian-based groups are often considered to be hiding places for rats, homosexuals, and child molesters. Muslim groups are more like gangs on the streets and are usually involved with various criminal activities. White religious groups like Wiccan and Ostetru are just cliques—guys looking for a group to hang out with. They wear symbols and talk about Thor being their god. The Native Americans are usually the most culturally true to their beliefs and are allowed to build sweat lodges in prison. Unfortunately, prison is prison, and young men are often sexually assaulted in the sweat lodges. There are also smaller religious groups like the Rastafarians, the Jews, the Mormons, the Jehovah Witnesses, etc.

More time is spent pursuing religion and sports than any other activity. If someone can find Jesus in any of these groups, awesome. But more often even the professing Christians in prison are not really dedicated to Jesus. It's just a safe place and a way to do their time.

Bible accounts clearly show that the Lord does not like cowardice in men or women. Spinelessness is repulsive to the kingdom of God. Jesus never called a soft or effeminate man to be a disciple. His followers were some of the roughest men of His day. A life of spiritual warfare is not a life for soft men. I apologize if it appears I am judging. I personally believe the reason the enemy can so easily destroy the children and young adults of America is because the leadership in the Christian church has grown soft and weak.

Many "Christians" that attend church in prison grew up in a Christian environment at home. When they became adults, they got involved with drugs or other criminal activity and ended up in prison. They know the tenets of religion well. This can be especially true of African-American men that were exposed to Christianity as children. Many of my buddies in prison learned religion by going to church with their mothers. They didn't know Jesus, but they knew religion.

EXTRAORDINARY SOLITUDE

Then there were a few guys like me who didn't grow up in church and knew nothing of religion. For months after being born again, I took communion before every single meal. I thought the Bible said we are to do that every time we remember Jesus. I was so hungry to know God that I would listen to anyone—even those with incorrect doctrine. God was merciful and protected my mind from cultish doctrines.

He also put the right people in my path. I met a Black Christian man who loaned me a Kenneth E. Hagin Study Bible. I got a job in the commissary and met a guy who had a box full of books by Kenneth E. Hagin, John G. Lake, and other Pentecostal leaders. My knowledge of Jesus was growing, but I felt there was so much more. I needed to hear from the Lord. I needed to know Him better.

What happened next may well be the most awesome experience of my life. I had been at Coleman for about nine months and had made a couple Christian friends in my unit with whom I read the Word and studied. One evening at mail call, I received a letter about the baptism in the Holy Spirit from Kenneth Copeland Ministries whose ministry reaches into prisons with the gospel. I looked up every scripture on how to receive the baptism of the Holy Spirit. A boldness came over me, and I showed my friend, Aaron, the letter. He had spent time around Full-Gospel believers and was already familiar with the baptism. I prayed so boldly right there in that prison cell that I was actually demanding that God baptize me in His Spirit, saying I was His child and that the Holy Spirit was as much for me as He was for anyone else.

Nothing seemed to happen, and I went back to my cell. The next day I headed for Aaron's cell so we could go to the chow hall together for lunch. Everyone else had already left and, as I paced in front of Aaron's cell, I received an impression in my spirit that I should open my mouth and let my tongue loose. This didn't make sense to me, but I obeyed. Immediately, my stomach began to stir. Something flew out of my belly and then up and out of my mouth! Tongues! I had received the baptism in the Holy Spirit! The tongues were coming fast and furious, and I walked quickly back to my cell and closed the door. I hit my knees and let the tongues fly for several minutes. Then I got the revelation and proclaimed, "Jesus, I knew You were there!"

Bear in mind that I had no church background—only the scriptures and the books I'd read. I would stand in front of the mirror, slow the tongues down, and try to interpret what was coming out of my mouth for a few minutes. I thought I had it. (I now know that isn't how it works.) Charged up, I found Aaron so he could hear my new prayer language. He had witnessed Christians receiving the Holy Spirit before and confirmed that I had been baptized in the Spirt and was speaking in tongues. Elated, I skipped chow and found my way to the chapel. I wanted to pray and do something—anything—for God.

Steven, after receiving the baptism of the Holy Spirit, with his friend, Aaron, at Coleman

A volunteer, a Black Baptist preacher from the streets, had come to the chapel to minister. I told him everything that had happened, and he asked me to step outside. He spoke quietly, in almost a whisper.

"The place where I preach on the street, we don't believe in that. But I have to tell you the truth. I was praying in my closet and God gave me the same thing."

Brothers and sisters, that is no exaggeration. We prayed right there—in a United States Federal

EXTRAORDINARY SOLITUDE

Prison—in tongues! A Baptist preacher who wasn't allowed to preach on baptism in the Holy Ghost and a career criminal. Amazing. Someone rolled by in a wheelchair, and the preacher and I prayed for him. I had entered a new level with the Lord.

Not long after, my roommate was transferred, and I was assigned a new cellmate, Guillermo—the Cuban high priest of Santeria. Santeria is an Afro-Caribbean religion that grew out of the Cuban slave trade and was based on the beliefs and traditions of Yoruba (a West-African ethnic group), along with some Catholic elements. Guillermo had photos of himself wearing religious garments with men standing all around him. He set up cards with pictures of idols above his bed. I prayed in tongues whenever he left the cell. After three days of this, I came back to the cell after work and found he was moving out. He said, through a translator, that he couldn't function in that cell. His body had locked up, and he couldn't even have a bowel movement in the room. I offered to let him have the cell, as I hoped to move in with Aaron, but he refused. He claimed he had been sick since the day he moved in.

As the weeks and months flowed by, I continued praying and studying the Word of God. I told the Christian community about my experience. Some were happy, some were confused, and some were jealous. I learned that everyone wasn't as hungry for God as I. Aaron and I became cell mates, which was a blessing in more than one way. He had money, and he looked out for me, especially regarding food. I played handball for exercise, and it became my athletic passion.

After many months, Aaron left the prison, and I was compelled to live with a grumpy old Black man named Jasper. Whites and Blacks don't typically live together in prison, but I had thrown politics out the window. I love Jesus and would take any opportunity to help someone or spread the gospel. Race didn't matter to me and neither did hurting the feelings of those playing prison politics. Unless the rule on the yard was that Blacks and whites could not live together, I would go where the Lord sent me.

I came back to my cell after working at Unicor, the prison factory, ready to relax. Climbing onto the top bunk, I settled in to read my Bible. One of Jasper's friends, a younger Black man who was very large and very loud, was in our cell and said something disrespectful to me on his way out.

I must be honest with you. I was still a baby Christian at this point and wasn't mature enough to let it go. Jumping off my bunk, I told Jasper I was going to go after his friend and beat him up. I blamed Jasper and told him it was his job to keep that man from disrespecting me, especially in my own cell. I put on my shoes, but I had cooled off a bit. Instead of attacking him, I gave him a chance to apologize for being disrespectful to me. But when he opened his mouth and his first word was not part of an apology, I punched him in front of several hundred men. A fight ensued, and I pummeled him again and again until the guards intervened. We were both taken to the SHU—Special Housing Unit—which is solitary confinement in the federal system. Trust me, there's nothing special about it.

Once I entered the SHU, I was placed into Administrative Detention where I would live until my hearing regarding the fight. Miguel, my roommate, was an absolute maniac from Mexico who was totally bound up by demons. He was never allowed a moment of rest but would stand on the sink for hours, yelling through the vent to the other members of his gang. Sometimes he would instruct them to clog their toilets and flush continuously so water would pour beneath the cell doors and flood the entire range.

During all this, I relaxed in my bunk, reading the Bible and listening to music on my headphones. After a few days, he starting asking questions about my faith. I suggested he read my Bible whenever I was listening to the radio and recommended that he begin with the Gospel of John. On the second night, I heard him crying and asked if everything was cool. He pointed to the scripture where Jesus was speaking to the Samaritan woman at the well. He told her that whoever drank of the water He was offering would never thirst again.

"I never read anything like that before," Miguel said, tears still streaming down his face.

EXTRAORDINARY SOLITUDE

I wasted no time in explaining the gospel to him, and he gave his heart to the Lord right there. Like all cells in modern prison SHUs, ours had a shower. I told him about baptism, and he asked if I could baptize him. I'd never heard of this being done in a prison shower, but if he was willing, so was I. God calls the shots. Amazing. One night, in a solitary confinement cell in Florida, a man who had never been fully exposed to the gospel, got saved and baptized! Hallelujah!

During the hearing over the fight, I was found guilty and confined to a special disciplinary wing of the SHU. The guards took me to an empty cell and shut the door. Handcuffed behind my back, I turned for the cuffs to be removed. Instead, I was told to step to the back of the cell. The door opened again, and guards ushered in Brunky, my roommate. White pieces of bone stuck out of both cheeks and through the bottom of his nostrils. With his back to the door, he thrust his wrists out of the slide so the cops could take off his cuffs. Released, he reached into his waistband and pulled out a 10-inch knife. I looked him dead in his eyes, as he sidestepped past me to the back of the cell. I was next and turned my back to the door, eager for my cuffs to be removed. The cop walked off without seeing the knife or the implied threat.

Brunky hid the knife under the mattress on the top bunk. "You are a Christian," he said bluntly. It was a statement, not a question.

Surprised, I replied, "Yes, I'm a Christian. How could you know that? I'm in here for fighting."

"I'm a devil worshiper. A real one. I could feel vibrations in my body when I walked into this cell. The vibrations are because of the Spirit that is in you." He explained he had several prominent books on witchcraft and demonic worship. His goal had been to be incarcerated in the highest security federal prison and move up the ranks of devil preachers in the Federal Bureau of Prisons.

Later that day, I suggested we make a deal. I would read aloud chapters from both his satanic bible and from the New Testament. He asked why I wasn't afraid to read the words in his bible. I explained that I wasn't afraid of anything, as I was protected by the blood of Jesus.

After a couple of weeks of reading several chapters a day, he said, "Hey, Rooster, no need to read out of my books anymore. Just keep reading out loud from your Bible." Speaking the Word out loud cuts to the heart.

Brunky was adamant that I never touch him under any circumstances. I couldn't imagine a scenario in which I would touch him unless he needed CPR. If he was asleep and the guards wanted him, he didn't want me to even tap his shoulder. I believe the spirits in him were terrified of the Spirit of God in me. I never saw Brunky give his heart to the Lord, but seeds were planted. Paul the Apostle says in 1

EXTRAORDINARY SOLITUDE

Corinthians 3:6-8 that one plants, another waters, and the Lord Himself gives the increase. I may never know what those seeds did, but God knows.

After my release from solitary, a few things had changed. First, I was suddenly a hero. The white people loved me. They lauded my fight as Black against white, with the white man crushing a Black man. I considered that viewpoint foolishness, and I refused to participate.

Once back in general population, I was placed in a different housing unit. Trying to stay in the Word was tough, as I had to deal with loud men in a crowded environment. Then God made another move, setting up a divine encounter that led to a friendship that would last for the rest of my life.

EXTRAORDINARY SOLITUDE

Chapter 9

A Divine Connection

*"Beloved, if any unholiness exists in the nature,
it is not there by the consent of the Spirit of God.
If unholiness is in your life it is because your soul is
giving consent to it, and you are retaining it.
Let it go.
Cast it out and let God have His way in your life."*
(John G. Lake)

Ages 27 to 32

José, a 60-year-old Puerto Rican, sat on the bleachers by the handball courts all day. Though he would play occasionally, he mostly just watched the games. And from time to time, he would talk to the players about Jesus.

Walking towards the handball courts a few days after I was released from solitary, I was surprised when José stepped into my path. We had never spoken before.

"I'm going to sow into your ministry," he said.

I almost laughed. "I don't have a ministry. I just got out of the SHU for fighting."

He nodded, almost as if he was pleased. "Good. It doesn't matter. The Lord spoke to me about you. I've already ordered the books you need—the best Christian books ever written."

And just like that, God sealed a divine appointment.

José—a friend for life

The books arrived just as José had promised. *God's Generals* by Roberts Liardon, books by Maria Woodworth-Etter, Kathryn Kuhlman, Smith Wigglesworth, John G. Lake, and other great leaders of the Church. It didn't take long for José and I to become close friends. I read the books cover to cover, asked tons of questions, then read them again. We walked the track for hours, discussing healing and miracles and the mysteries and wonder of the Holy Spirit. José knew a lot about such things having received the baptism in the Holy Spirit nearly 20 years before.

José became more than my spiritual mentor and took me under his wing in so many ways. He made sure I had at least $25 every month in my account and set me up with hand-me-down shoes from other inmates, so I could play handball. He cooked Puerto Rican dishes like Mofongo and let me eat for free. José loved Jesus with his whole heart. He was a true convert. No wimpy Christianity for José. He knew that Jesus chose a certain type of man to be an apostle. All, except for Judas, were tough men in their own way—and so was José. The man was real and didn't play games with Christianity. He was my best friend on the inside and our friendship remained true after he was released twelve years ago.

It wasn't unusual for José and me to be watching a softball game, and a fight would break out with the players chasing and hitting each other with baseball bats.

While there was no doubt I was saved and wanted to grow in my faith, I still had a tremendous number of issues regarding my character and personality. I could still lose my mind in frustration and anger when playing sports. If I thought a bad call was made against me, or if I wasn't playing well, I would go absolutely insane.

EXTRAORDINARY SOLITUDE

Gambling was also an issue. From time to time, I would make money playing chess. José never ever gave me a dressing down. He understood I was young both in age and in the faith and that my flaws were many. Instead, he urged me not to be too hard on myself. Even the most holy of Christians weren't perfect. He suggested that, rather than gambling on chess, perhaps I could earn money teaching other inmates how to play the game. I didn't think it would work, but he knew the Holy Spirit better than I did. He asked what I would charge for a one-hour lesson every day for a month—basically 30 lessons. I threw out the ridiculous price of $150. A guy in José's unit became my first client. I had clients waiting in line, ready to pay me $150 a month. This went on for a year.

* * *

Jessica was released from prison after serving twelve months. She wanted to save our marriage and moved to Florida, living with her father so she could be close to the prison. She visited me on a regular basis, bringing the kids along. I would pray in tongues as I approached the visiting room and then suddenly have the filthiest thoughts about having sex with her. How could this be? How could a Spirit-filled believer have anger, hate, lust, and all these other sinful thoughts? My flesh and my mind needed renewing. I saw this pattern in the Bible with Peter and some of the others.

The gifts of the Holy Spirit were operating in the believers in Corinth, yet Paul pointed out that they were becoming carnally minded. Didn't he say that he had been forsaken by certain brothers who had traveled with him? If a born-again, Spirit-filled believer could not fall, why are there so many warnings in the letters to the Church? It happens a lot, and it is ugly, and it is sad. But it happens—especially when the demonic is involved.

We all know how hard it is to overcome the flesh. Adding satanic influence to the mix is like throwing gasoline on a fire. Christians must be taught the basics of spiritual warfare. We must be able to protect ourselves and our families. We'll get into that later. For now, just know that you—as a believer—have been given authority over all demons. But you have to exercise this authority. You must bind the evil spirits, and you must rebuke them in the name of Jesus.

Jessica stayed strong for a couple of years. I noticed a change in the frequency of our visits. And then the visits stopped altogether. She would accept my phone calls, but she refused to see me. This is the inevitable life of a prisoner serving 20 years. No one can expect a spouse to wait that long. I encouraged her to move on with her life, but begged her to bring Steven to visit me.

One day, I called Jessica's house, and Steven, who was very young, answered the phone. He was supposed to have gone to the fair the night before, so I asked if he had fun.

"It wasn't very much fun because I didn't get to ride hardly any rides."

I smiled. "That's probably because you're too little to ride some of them."

"No Dad, it's not because I'm so little. It's because of the baby."

I was confused, and a feeling of dread crept over me. "What baby?"

"The baby that's in my mommy's belly."

Jessica was pregnant. Our relationship was never the same, even though I assured her I wasn't angry. I had told her to go on with her life and that's what she had done. But we were still officially married. I asked her to grant me a divorce. She was still young and pretty and the future could hold so much. She refused to divorce me, but she also refused to come back to the prison or to bring my son to visit me.

A few years after Jessica gave birth, she started dating a man who was a meth cook. She was badly burned in a meth lab explosion, and Steven was adopted by her mother.

I was saddened by the news that my former cell mate, Aaron, had died from pneumonia within a year of being released. He was in his early thirties, in great shape, and living a clean life. I firmly believe that the enemy took Aaron before his time.

José was getting close to his release date as well. He was finally going home after serving 20-plus years in federal prison for a non-violent drug crime. My world was changing at a time when I needed to stay especially close to Jesus—and I stumbled. Badly.

EXTRAORDINARY SOLITUDE

Pablo, a chess student from the Dominican Republic, was extremely wealthy and hired an attorney for me in an attempt to shave some time off my sentence. Ten of the twenty-two years of my federal sentence had been based on my prior marijuana conviction, for which I had originally received probation. Since that time, pot laws had become much more lenient, and I hoped this would be taken into consideration.

Pablo said he would pay me to study the stock market and teach him how to trade. He supplied all the educational books. I took studying the stock market seriously. Sadly, it became like the seed that was choked out by the cares of the world in Matthew 13:22: "Now he who received seed among the thorns is he who hears the word, and the cares of this world and the deceitfulness of riches choke the word, and he becomes unfruitful." My focus shifted to getting out of prison and studying the markets, and I began to take my eyes off the Lord, opening the door for the enemy to come back into my life.

Everything seemed to be headed in the right direction but was going the other way.

José was released. Aaron was dead. Upon his release, Pablo was deported back to the Dominican Republic. I only spoke to him a few times before he disappeared.

But God is God.

I was shocked to found out José was back. I never knew a man so close to Jesus, and, surely, he couldn't have committed another crime. His story was absolutely supernatural.

José had been sent to a halfway house in Miami, Florida. While there, he heard the voice of the Lord telling him to go back to prison. José had so much going for him upon his release. His wife had waited for over 20 years. His son, a multimillionaire, had already purchased a home and a vehicle for him. José had no idea why the Lord wanted him to go back to prison, but he was obedient.

He entered the holding facility and, when he reached his assigned cell, found a small Spanish man sitting on a bed. He was facing a long term, perhaps even a life sentence.

The man held up a Bible. "Do you know anything about this?" he asked José. "I have been praying for God to send someone who can explain it to me."

José had been sent there for that reason. Though saddened that José was back in prison, I was grateful for the opportunity to spend another six months with him.

* * *

A few months later, I was called to the prison receiving department and told to pack my belongings. Confused, I explained that I was comfortable at Coleman, where I had been for five years, and had not requested a transfer. What I wanted didn't matter. I was to pack my property immediately and prepare to be transported. Because of the sexual abuse case with

EXTRAORDINARY SOLITUDE

Susie, when she was 17 and I was 21, I was being sent to a prison in a pilot program within the federal system for sex offenders—even though I was in federal prison for trafficking drugs. Sex offenders? How in the world they put me in that category is beyond stupidity.

Upon my transfer, I was interviewed by the psychologist in charge of the program. He stated the obvious: I didn't belong there. I didn't meet the criteria, and I had a near-zero recidivism rate. That was great news, but it wouldn't get me back to Coleman, where I had settled in and was, as much as is possible, content. And so began my road trips to various federal prisons.

I began studying the men, the sex-offenders, surrounding me and would often interview them for hours on end, trying to get a handle on their thinking. These guys were not normal, even by prison standards. I came to believe that the only possible way a man could be sexually attracted to a small child was through the demonic. Regardless of what our culture today endorses, pedophilia is unnatural. Most of the molesters I spoke with had been molested themselves. I'm convinced this molestation was a contact point through which the demons were transferred. This condition cannot be cured through imprisonment, rehabilitation, or medication. Putting pedophiles behind bars does nothing to change this unnatural and immoral predilection. Only the power of the Holy Spirit and the authority of the name of Jesus can set these people free and deliver them from these evil thoughts.

EXTRAORDINARY SOLITUDE

Large groups of inmates from all four corners of the United States were thrown together at Marianna prison in Florida. Many were Hispanics imprisoned for rape or for molesting underage girls. Most of the child molesters were kidnappers or Internet paraphiles. There was a sprinkling of pimps and a few guys like me. When I saw the makeup of the prison populace, I knew trouble was coming. After being in multiple prisons for almost nine years, my experience was that, whenever the majority of the inmates hailed from different parts of the country, conflict brewed just below the surface. I was right. Before long, a massive riot broke out.

*Steven, P-Nut & Jack
Marianna, FL (2010)*

The riot lasted for almost twenty minutes with the guards helpless to rein in the inmates. I was in the rec yard when the riot happened, but I was blessed to be unharmed. All the prisoners involved were

Spanish. Many were stabbed, and I lost count of the pools of blood scattered around the yard.

While I knew Jesus was always with me, I found it more and more difficult to spend time praying and studying the Word. Instead, I allowed myself to be distracted by all that was going on around me. Guilt about my lack of dedication to God weighed me down. Satan loves the heaviness of condemnation and is pleased when we feel unworthy and guilty. Born-again believers remain in right standing with God because of the blood of Jesus. If we sin, even if we sin thousands of times, we need only return to God and repent. The Lord is always faithful to forgive. A true repentant broken spirit brings Jesus on the scene instantly. He loves us. He truly does.

At this time of my life, I failed to confess my sins before God and turn to Him . . . and Satan nearly killed me.

EXTRAORDINARY SOLITUDE

Chapter 10

The Valley of the Shadow

*"There is nothing impossible with God.
All the impossibility is with us when we measure
God by the limitations of our unbelief."*
(Smith Wigglesworth)

Ages 33 to 40

I woke up drenched in sweat. Not feeling well, I drank fluids and rested for a couple of days but grew weaker and weaker. On the third day, I dragged myself to medical. They ran a few tests and concluded nothing was wrong. The next day I developed a hacking cough and felt even worse. A few days later I was in a wheelchair, too weak to walk. Jack, my roommate, wheeled me back to medical, and I explained the symptoms I was experiencing. So weak I couldn't give a firm handshake, I sweat profusely through the night and coughed persistently. My body was strong and muscular as I had worked out five days a week for seven years. Now I couldn't even walk.

A doctor examined an x-ray and said my lungs looked as though I had been smoking large amounts of marijuana. What?! I hadn't smoked any type of drug in seven years. I was sent back to my unit to die. Literally.

The next day Jack wheeled me to a lieutenant. So weak I could barely speak, I wrote down my symptoms. He sent me back to medical who once again sent me back to my unit. The next morning, the medical staff found me and frantically asked how I was feeling. I felt like I was dying. They confirmed my fear. I was dying. My lungs had filled with fluid, and I was suffering from severe pneumonia.

This was the same sickness that had killed my Christian brother Aaron right after he was released from prison. He was only 33 years old. And I was 33 years old. We were both children of God who had served Him even though we were living in the chaos and depravity of a prison. We had disrupted the kingdom of darkness. Even so, the moment we failed to walk hand-in-hand with the Lord, we dropped our shields, and the enemy attacked us, intending to kill us and put an end to our testimonies. I believe this happens many times throughout the Christian life. Jesus warned us, as did Peter and Paul, that the enemy is always on the prowl, seeking whom he may devour.

EXTRAORDINARY SOLITUDE

A dedicated Christian scares Satan. But this isn't a game. Once we leap into spiritual warfare and cause serious damage to the kingdom of darkness, we cannot step out from under the covering of the Lord Jesus. Doing so opens a door to the enemy, and he will do what he can—whether it be sickness or disease, loss of loved ones, financial calamity, whatever--and try to kill or destroy you.

After a week of daily antibiotic injections, I began to recover and, slowly but surely, improved significantly in the following month. I worked out harder and harder to rebuild my lung capacity, eventually getting back to a hundred percent.

Soon after I regained my health, I was transferred to another prison in Butner, North Carolina. The change would do me good. While I knew God was with me and I only had to cry out to Him, I still carried the shame of allowing myself to be drawn away from Him by the "cares of the world." This burden of guilt made it difficult for me to share my testimony. I had to find my way back, but I didn't know where to start. Being able to talk to José by phone was a blessing. But walking with God is an individual decision. The Word says in 1 Samuel 15:23, ***"For rebellion is as the sin of witchcraft, and stubbornness is as iniquity . . ."***

The Lord had healed my body and saved me from certain death. Could I find my way back and walk with Him daily as I once had? What would happen if I didn't?

*　*　*

Walking on the compound at Butner was almost like getting out of prison. Federal prisons have four basic security levels from highest to lowest: penitentiary, medium, low, and camp. The Illinois state prison system is similar. I had served time in two penitentiaries and two medium-security facilities in Illinois. In the federal system I had been in two medium-highs. Butner was a low-security prison, which was a drastic change from any other prison I had experienced. The most radical difference was that the living quarters were dorms, unlike the cells in penitentiaries and mediums. This took months to get used to. But the lack of respect among the inmates was the hardest difference to grasp.

Butner didn't have an atmosphere of danger, so most of the soft inmates took the liberty to act tough. There was also a lack of common prison courtesy. Civilities, such as excuse me, pardon me, thank you, you're welcome, etc., were rarely uttered. In high-level prisons, these phrases are always used because every inmate is a potential killer.

Butner was a different world, and my prison life changed the moment I walked into the recreation yard. Having gambled heavily on pool when I was on the street, my eyes widened at the sight of a huge room filled with nine-foot pool tables. An inmate named Burr had been a semiprofessional pool player before his incarceration and served as a pool instructor, teaching table maintenance and billiards in all forms.

Pool room—Butner, NC (2013)

I practically lived in that pool hall for the next two years. Under Burr's tutelage, I studied billiards as though I planned to become a professional pool player. We became good friends, and I eventually became his assistant instructor. I got a job working on the pool tables and spent most of my free time there. My skill rose to a competitive level, and I began making some decent money gambling. I beat guys from all over the country. I was good, and my opponents knew that coming into the contest. Though he never asked, I gave Burr a cut of whatever I won. He had taught me a lot and deserved a piece of the action.

EXTRAORDINARY SOLITUDE

Where was God during this time? As always, Jesus stood at the door and knocked. But, in my shame and guilt, I continued to shut Him out.

A new inmate named Mike moved to my unit, and we became good friends. He was about my age and, together, we worked out during the day and made wine at night. He was a good guy from a good family. Like me, he got involved in the drug business and got caught. Upon waking every morning, Mike read and studied his Bible. And I would turn and walk away. How could I explain how close I had been to God, how I had been baptized in the Holy Spirit, and now I'm making wine and gambling for a living in prison?

I had so much freedom at Butner, it was almost as if I had been released from prison. I played and coached softball, kept up a rigorous workout routine, and competed in prison CrossFit competitions. Everyday existence was comfortable.

During the third year, Billy Mac, a pool shark and professional poker player, transferred to Butner for cancer treatment. Under his tutelage, I became proficient at No Limit Hold 'em and Omaha Poker and added my winnings to my monthly income. Unlike most inmates, I didn't have money sent to me from family or friends on the outside. Chopper had sent me $50 or $60 a week for many years, but those funds were unreliable as he would get into trouble, go to jail, or lose his job. Playing pool or poker for money provided a consistent income. I realized later that this,

EXTRAORDINARY SOLITUDE

too, was evidence that I wasn't trusting God. There's no doubt the Lord would have provided for me, but I took it upon myself to make my own way and not rely on the One who had promised to provide all my needs.

Improving your skill at pool doesn't cost anything. You just have to practice. Poker is different. Gambling is the only way to get better at poker. Because I didn't have the money to do this, I put aside my pride and stood behind Billy Mac, watching as he played, ignoring the laughs and jokes. I didn't care. I had a plan and was determined to develop a skill. When I transferred to another prison and took my new set of skills with me, I played poker for a living. I won $1,100 on my best day—a lot of money in prison. My winnings paid my commissary bill for months.

The world would say I was doing great, considering I was in prison, but I was falling further away from the Lord every day. The enemy's claws dug deeper and deeper, and I didn't even notice what was happening. That's one of his best tricks. Before we realize we're drowning, we're lying on the bottom of the pond. My thinking was deteriorating to almost the same level it had been when I was on the street. The only thing missing was alcohol. The demons needed gasoline.

Society has many misconceptions about prison, including the belief that prisoners spend time thinking about their crimes and the harm they've done. There's time to think while you're in jail, waiting

EXTRAORDINARY SOLITUDE

for your trial. Prison is different. Convicts purposefully fill their days with activity. An inmate can become so busy that there's barely time to call their families. A typical day might look like this:

6AM	Wake up and a shower
6:30AM	Breakfast
7AM	Drink coffee
7:30AM	Go to work
8-11AM	Work
11AM	Lunch
11:30AM	Return to work
12--3:30PM	Work
3:30—4:30PM	Lockdown for count followed by a nap.
4:30PM	Dinner
5:30—8PM	Free time: watch TV, play sports, work out
8PM	After-workout meal
9PM	Shower
9:30PM	Lockdown

An inmate would repeat the same schedule every day. I filled my days with billiards, poker, and working out with a little softball or a game of chess from time to time. Spending time with the Lord wasn't part of my routine. I was occupied with the things of the world, and I received the world's reward.

Going into my fourth year at Butner prison, Mike transferred to a camp, and I was involved in another fight. While I cleaned pool tables, I got into an argument. The quarrel escalated, and we moved to a room mainly used for music. He took a swing at me and missed. I did not. The fight was over in about 10 seconds, and the result was horrifying. The situation looked bad for me, so I punched myself twice in the face to make the fight appear to be in self-defense. The guards took me to solitary confinement. The other guy was taken to an outside medical facility.

Instead of walking closely with the Lord, I allowed my flesh with its flaws of anger and rage to surface. My life with the Spirit was broken, and the fruits that so define the Christian life were not evident.

After spending a couple of months in solitary confinement, I was transferred yet again, this time to a medium-security prison in Virginia. Like Butner, the prison basically ran itself. Petersburg, however, had easier access to alcohol and drugs. While they're available at every prison, some are more flooded than others. I fell in right where I left off in Butner—gambling at pool, poker, and chess. Every debauchery accelerated, and I was rushing full speed ahead toward death.

My once-cherished books had transferred with me several times, but I gave them all to a Christian in Petersburg. I kept my Bible, storing it at the bottom of my locker under my poker books. After about eighteen months, the guards pulled me out of my cell, saying I was under investigation and placed me in solitary confinement. "Under investigation" is a code phrase meaning they didn't have to give me a reason. I was transferred—again—three months later, this time to Marion Illinois Federal Prison. Wouldn't you think I would stop and reach out to God at some point? Perhaps if I had prayed just once, I could have saved myself from the pain lying in wait for me. His plan for me would have come to pass, and no weapon formed against me would prosper (Isaiah 54:17).

But I didn't.

Marion is a medium-security prison that had once been a penitentiary. The only advantage was that it was closer to my family. After thirteen years in federal prison, I was finally back in my home state. Aunt Marsha and Chopper visited fairly often, which helped a bit. The prison itself was in appalling condition. The recreation area was abysmal, and the inmates were foul and disrespectful like the men I had encountered at Butner. Every inmate was required to live in a three-man cell for at least a year—a stupid rule that's unheard of in the Federal Bureau of Prisons.

I didn't last a year at Marion. Under investigation again, this time for introducing contraband, I was confined to the SHU on May 10, 2017. I was still in solitary on March 15, 2018, when I sat down to write this book. During the year spent in solitary confinement, so many miracles, salvations, and baptisms were happening all around me, and I felt compelled by the Holy Spirit to write. How God reveals Himself in our darkest hour many times depends on us. If we turn back to Him, He welcomes us with open arms.

Most are familiar with the parable of the Prodigal Son in Luke 15:11-24. The Prodigal didn't return to his father the moment he went broke and was living a life of debauchery. He waited until he was starving to death. Eating with the swine. Meanwhile, his father watched the horizon every day and waited in hope that his son would come home. When he finally saw his prodigal son approaching, did his father turn his back? Did he tell him he'd gotten what he deserved, that he'd made his bed and had to lie in it? No. When he saw his son a long way off, he ran to him with his arms wide open.

Just like God did for me.

EXTRAORDINARY SOLITUDE

Between the Chapters

The Apostle Peter walked with the Lord for over three years. He saw miracles and walked on water with Jesus. Yet he still cut off the ear of a man who put his hand on Jesus. I again opened the door to the enemy. In Matthew 12:43-45, Jesus explained to His disciples that, after a demon spirit is cast out of an individual, he goes to dry places. Then, returning to the home he had been cast out of and finding it swept and clean, he brings with him seven more spirits more wicked than he.

God created me with a mind and a determination to accomplish anything—when I was sober. For the past several years, I had been wasting my talents. I needed God more than ever, but I was too ashamed to turn back to Him. The Bible gives us several reasons why this can be so. In Genesis 4:7, God told Cain, "Sin lies at the door and its desire is for you, but you should rule over it." Sin was undeniably at my door. Revelation 3:20 tells us Jesus is at the door, too. ***"Behold, I stand at the door and knock. If anyone hears My voice and opens the door, I will come in to him and dine with him, and he***

with Me. " We serve whoever—or whatever—we let in.

Galatians 6:1a reveals that even believers can be overtaken in any trespass (sin). ***"Brethren, if a man is overtaken in any trespass . . . "*** Once we open the door to the enemy to fulfill the lust of the flesh, we can either repent and return to the Lord, or we are overtaken in that sin. I could not be possessed by a demon because I had been born again, but I was being demonized—oppressed by demons. I needed deliverance, but I didn't know how to shake off the shackles that had me bound.

Galatians 6:1 continues, saying, ***"You who are spiritual restore such a one . . . "*** But who is spiritual in prison? Half of the Church in America doesn't believe in the gifts of the Spirit, divine healing, or deliverance. How much more difficult it is to find a true believer in prison. While I am not a theologian and I haven't attended seminary, I know for certain that Jesus can deliver you the way He delivered me.

EXTRAORDINARY SOLITUDE

EXTRAORDINARY SOLITUDE

Part Three
Return

EXTRAORDINARY SOLITUDE

Chapter 11

Heading for Home

"A man is in a great place when he has no one to turn to but God."
(Smith Wigglesworth)

May 10, 2017

In early May 2017, I was placed in the hole for introducing contraband to the prison population. I had been selling an opioid blocker called Suboxone to the heroin addicts. Yes, I wanted to make extra money, but there was more to my decision to make Suboxone available. The federal prisons were in the midst of a heroin-overdose epidemic. No plan was in place to deal with the fentanyl-laced heroin or the massive overdoses the drug was producing. An addict taking Suboxone will get violently ill if he uses heroin or fentanyl. I think it's interesting to note that five years after I was put in detention for introducing

EXTRAORDINARY SOLITUDE

Suboxone, the federal prisons began prescribing it to inmates.

Every unit of solitary confinement in the federal system is unique, but they are all called SHUs. At Marion, I was confined to an SHU with bar doors instead of steel doors, which made the solitary confinement experience loud and noisy. I had a roommate and a deck of homemade playing cards made from the sides of paper milk cartons. The only property allowed was a radio and shower shoes.

When the property officer showed up at my cell door, she brought something extra—my old Bible. I didn't touch the Bible for the first month and was starting to feel a bit depressed. Out of the blue, an officer asked if I wanted to be an orderly in the SHU. The coveted position would allow me to leave my cell for a few hours each day to sweep and mop the hallways. I would also have access to extra food. I eagerly accepted the offer but was told to be patient until he could get approval from a higher-ranking officer. Unfortunately, I was denied the orderly job—and any other job—because I had tried to introduce Suboxone strips.

My roommate went home after a month or so, and I moved to a single-man cell, which I preferred. I began reading a few scriptures a day and took a critical look at myself and who I had become. When I finally came to the Lord in prayer, it dawned on me that I had not prayed in years. Could I still pray? Could I still pray in tongues? In Romans 11:29, the Word tells us, *"**For the gifts and the calling of God are irrevocable.**"* I confessed that Scripture, determined to embrace that gift once again. The tongues returned, slowly at first, and some months passed before the Holy Spirit flowed easily off my lips. But He was still there! Most of my prayers were geared towards repentance. I would tell the Lord I wasn't praying to get out of trouble. I asked that all my prayers be about drawing back to Him.

José (2017)

For years my friend José and I had kept in touch through email. Since I was in the SHU, we had to go back to pen and paper. My pen couldn't be longer than three inches and had a soft, flexible casing. After a couple of weeks of striving to draw nearer to God, I wrote to José. José was a true Christian friend and would have stayed in contact with me even if I had killed five people. News of my stepping toward the Lord again had to make him smile.

EXTRAORDINARY SOLITUDE

Just before I was confined to solitary, José's son gave him a huge stack of stamps. José had no need for even one stamp. Neither of us had any idea that I would end up in solitary confinement for over a year. Only the worst offenders who stabbed someone or assaulted a staff member spent over a year in solitary. Such a punishment is never inflicted on a non-violent contraband offender like me. But God always has a plan. He knew how long I needed to be confined in the SHU to be alone with Him.

Early on, I noticed the prison chaplain making his rounds. He came by once a week, so I stopped him the next week. I was a bit skeptical because the staff members who claimed to be Christians were predominately weak in their faith. Sadly, this included prison chaplains. A few tried to be effective, but many were just going through the motions, seeing the chaplaincy as an easy nine-to-five job. Thankfully, the chaplain at Marion was totally sold out for Jesus. He was Full Gospel and grew up in an Assembly of God Church.

He was allowed to bring one book per week per inmate. He had a book list, and I could request whatever book I wanted to read. He reached into his cart and pulled out a book on generational curses. That was the first book I read in the SHU. I eventually took advantage of the one book per inmate rule by getting other inmates to request books for me. I spent the next eleven months alone with God.

EXTRAORDINARY SOLITUDE

EXTRAORDINARY SOLITUDE

Chapter 12

Going Deeper, Growing Stronger

"How do you move on?
You move on when your heart finally
understands that there is no turning back."
(J. R. R. Tolkien)

After about three months in the SHU, a burden from the Lord was on me, and I intensified my time with Him. I prayed and read the Word for longer periods and listened only to Christian music, though I did allow myself to listen to the Cubs' games. I read every Christian book I could get my hands on, some of them two or three times. One day, I was on my knees praying in the Spirit. After about fifteen minutes, I started crying and eventually I prayed through to Heaven. There are times when it seems as if our prayers are hitting on a brass ceiling and cannot get through to God. We must press through during these times. Jesus said that the kingdom of Heaven suffers violence, and it must be taken by force. Not physical force, spiritual force. But this was something different.

With tears on my cheeks and snot running out of my nose, I asked God what had just happened. He clearly said, "The devil has been trying to kill you." That was it. He added nothing else. It was enough! Not long after, I stopped listening to Cubs baseball and focused all my energy on prayer and reading the Word and Spirit-filled books. I listened only to Christian music and the most powerful Christian men and women who were on the radio.

José wrote to me at least twice a week, using those stamps his son had given him. He also sent me some excellent books, and I discussed them with him and the chaplain. I had read some of the authors years earlier. Iron sharpens iron and their words of encouragement, correction, and faith sharpened my spirit. Authors like Smith Wigglesworth, Charles and Frances Hunter, Kenneth E. Hagin, Dutch Sheets, Gordon Lindsay, Derek Prince, Merlin Carothers, Pat Brooks, Myles Munroe, John Wimber, Dennis Bennett, and many others. When I become determined, it is always to the extreme. The Lord put a fire in me to focus on receiving all of God. I wanted everything the Lord had for me—everything He had given these authors.

How could I become the most effective witness for Christ? How could I help others who had been through something similar? The only way was to press in for all the tools the Lord has made available. My heart's desire was to be fully equipped to help others, specifically those who had traveled the darkest roads. But gifts have a cost. Was I willing to pay that cost?

José sent me a letter about seeds—not the seeds we sow in the ground, but the seeds God plants in our hearts. The Holy Spirit prompted me to examine the seeds inside the core of the apple I was going to eat. After eating the apple, I opened the core and discovered a large diamond! Oval shaped and sparkling, the diamond was suspended inside the core. I stared at it for a few minutes, then tried to pull it out. My fingers were too big, so I hit it with a plastic fork. The diamond broke apart into nothing and vanished. I understood that the Lord was letting me know I was on the right path. This was the beginning of the Holy Spirit revealing Himself through amazing signs and wonders.

After eating lunch about a week later, I rose from my little desk to wash my hands. I realized something was missing from my tray. I yelled to my neighbors, asking what food items were on their trays.

The main dish was eggs. I wasn't served eggs. I prayed, "Lord, you always bless me, but today I did not get my eggs." Perhaps someone else was hungrier than I and the Lord had met his need by giving him a double portion of eggs. Moving to the front of my cell, I looked down. Against the outside bars lay a big, green apple! Bending down, I picked up the apple to find a cross bruised perfectly onto it. Amazing! I showed the apple to my neighbors and to the guard. This was definitely God being God. It was time to take my life with the Lord to another level, but I didn't know how. Everything would soon be revealed to me.

Author and preacher Derek Prince walked in the supernatural gifts of the Holy Spirit and was also a gifted teacher. Those talents do not always coincide. God used John Alexander Dowie and William Branham to perform thousands of miracles, including creative miracles of healing, yet they were not gifted as teachers or preachers. Derek Prince was effective in teaching others to walk in the supernatural. I had seen a few of his videos while I was incarcerated in Coleman prison years earlier. In one video, he cast a demon out of an elderly woman who had been dabbling in horoscopes.

When I scanned the list of books available from the chaplain, I saw only one book available by Derek Prince. That book was about fasting. In my early Christian walk, I had only fasted one time, right after I was born again. In this book, Derek Prince wrote about fasting as a way of life. He taught that fasting for long periods of time was a spiritual weapon and a way to receive breakthroughs.

Although Derek Prince said the length of the fast wasn't the most important thing, he thought a seven-day fast would change the course of a person's life. I believed every word he said. I didn't really know how to fast for one day, let alone seven. That's a long fast! Prince had fasted for 21 days and his wife for 28 days. Isaiah 58:6-12 instructs us to use fasting as a tool and a weapon against the enemy.

This led me to fast as a routine. Beginning with one day a week, I built myself up to fasting three days a week. After about five weeks, I tried a seven-day fast and focused on spiritual gifts. To be honest, I am fairly thin and losing fifteen pounds in seven days was agonizing, but God gave me grace, and I was able to complete the fast.

While praying in tongues near the end of day two, I became aware that both my prayer language and my facial expression were changing. It seemed like the Spirit was bursting out of me. I received a much faster prayer language, and I could not stop smiling. This has been my main prayer language ever since, and I am still smiling! From that point forward I fasted a minimum of one day a week. Sometimes I would fast two days until 4PM. I again fasted seven days about six months later.

Let me be clear. A person cannot just give their life to Jesus, fast for a month, and walk around with spiritual power. That's not how it works. While I can testify that praying while fasting is like lifting weights on steroids, I cannot claim to be an expert on fasting. I only know that fasting has improved my relationship with the Lord Jesus and opened the spiritual realm to allow me to be a powerful man of God. He has granted me incredible answers to prayer. Praying in tongues combined with fasting unlocks a different dimension to your life with Jesus.

Be sure to consult a physician and get clearance before fasting. Focus your fast. Have a specific reason for fasting. For example, you can fast for answered prayers. You can fast to draw near to God. You can fast to be rewarded by God. All of these are good Biblical reasons. Let's take a moment and review a few scriptures to bear in mind while fasting:

"Moreover, when you fast, do not be like the hypocrites, with a sad countenance. For they disfigure their faces that they may appear to men to be fasting. Assuredly, I say to you, they have their reward. But you, when you fast, anoint your head and wash your face, so that you do not appear to men to be fasting, but to your Father who is in the secret place; and your Father who sees in secret will reward you openly." (Matthew 6:16-18)

"But without faith it is impossible to please Him, for he who comes to God must believe that He is, and that He is a rewarder of those who diligently seek Him." (Hebrews 11:6)

"Draw near to God and He will draw near to you. Cleanse your hands, you sinners;

and purify your hearts, you double-minded." (James 4:8)

(Referring to evil spirits) *"However, this kind does not go out except by prayer and fasting."* (Matthew 17:21)

Now that my prayer language was flowing like never before, the Lord placed a Kenneth E. Hagin book in my hands that I had read years before. Hagin wrote about a period in his life when he prayed in tongues for five hours a day. During those months, the Lord gave him a spirit of wisdom and revelation. Desiring those same gifts, I prayed in the spirit for five hours every day for several weeks. Eventually I reduced this to three hours a day, and then to one continuous hour by the end of my time in solitary confinement. Of course, I prayed in tongues when prompted by the Holy Spirit and in English as I needed. But I always made time for at least one hour of continuous prayer. This opened a new level of spiritual revelation and knowledge that included dreams and visions.

We cannot attach a formula to God. He doesn't work that way. This is just what worked for me and has worked for other men of God throughout history. In my experience, I have yet to see a life of fasting and prayer that did not produce fruit. It is all about taking steps towards God.

EXTRAORDINARY SOLITUDE

The chaplain always gave me the perfect books at the perfect moments. On two occasions the chaplain brought me books I hadn't ordered because the books I had requested were not available. Both times, the books were perfect for what I had been praying about. God always provides answers.

Distance is never an issue with the Holy Spirit. He is omniscient—everywhere at all times. The Lord could give me a dream in Illinois and give my friend José the exact same dream in Florida. There are no limits for God unless we limit Him in our lives by our lack of faith.

God led me to heart-wrenching repentance. To a life completely saturated in His Word. To hours of prayer and days of fasting. And He always ensured that I had the most powerful Christian books written by truly God-centered men and women. Yet one thing remained: I had to get clean from the garbage I had picked up and allowed in my house. Yes, I'm talking about being delivered from demonic oppression. Yes, I was born again. Yes, I was full of the Holy Spirit of God. And yes, I was seeing God do supernatural miracles in my life. But I was still being hounded by demons and demonic influences I had allowed to create strongholds in my mind. I had invited them into my life, and I was the one responsible for getting rid of them. I needed to learn how to do that correctly. I didn't know I had these things in me or around me, but I wasn't completely surprised when I realized I did. I knew that my mind didn't always function correctly, and I had the most horrible thoughts. I sensed the presence of a force that was not of God. So, how did I finally figure out what was going on?

God put the right book in my hands at precisely the right time.

This book was written by Pat Brooks, a woman who had been mentored by Don Basham and Lester Sumrall. Basham and Sumrall led world-famous deliverance ministries before it became a kooky sideshow. They worked in third-world countries where the demonic was running rampant, battling voodoo priests and extreme forms of demonic influence in Asia and Africa. That book had been passed from one generation to another and had now been passed to me. I applied the teachings to my own life and modeled the prayers into personal ones. Fasting for long periods and praying those prayers changed the course of my life.

If you are suffering from demonic oppression, you can pray these prayers over yourself to gain freedom. This is not a magic formula. You must be desperate to be free and use these biblical prayers as a weapon. I did not have a minister to help me find deliverance. I was able to attain it on my own through the Lord Jesus. You also can get deliverance on your own through Jesus. I promise you this will work no matter how bound you have been by the enemy or immersed in the demonic life you have been. These prayers have been edited somewhat along the lines of repentance. I open every prayer by asking the Lord to forgive me for my sins as I forgive any who have sinned against me. I release them, and I hold nothing against them. I ask the Lord to release me from my sins and to forgive me in Jesus' name. I open every prayer that way.

These are the steps I followed to gain deliverance:

Step #1—Renouncing Satan

Begin by renouncing out loud any supernatural experience in your life that is not of God. Ask Jesus to close your personality to that realm. In His name, renounce hypnotism, Ouija boards, spiritualism, reincarnation, ESP, palm reading, astrology, and horoscopes, witchcraft, sorcery—everything psychic or connected to the occult. Renounce anything that denies the blood of Jesus Christ and every philosophy that denies His divinity. Call upon Jesus to set you free.

Step #2—Forgiving Others

Forgive others, praying something like this, "Lord Jesus, I've hated certain people and have held bitterness and resentment against them. I am sorry, and I will myself to forgive them. I want your help, Jesus. Please bring to mind the names of those I need to forgive. I forgive everyone I've hated and held a grudge against. If I've forgotten someone, I forgive them. As it says in Your Word, I ask you to forgive me as I forgive them. Thank You, Lord, for forgiving me and for releasing me from all guilt and condemnation."

Step #3—Prayer of Confession of Faith

Say a prayer similar to this: "I believe I am a child of God saved by the grace of Jesus Christ. I know He died on the cross for me; I know He shed his blood for my sins; I receive Jesus as my Lord and Savior. I commit my life to Him and hereby renounce all the works of Satan. I renounce every evil spirit that binds or torments me. In the name of Jesus Christ, I renounce them all and call upon the Lord to set me free. Amen."

Step #4—Attacking the Spirits

To take authority over any evil spirit that is oppressing you, you must verbally attack the spirits. If you know what the spirit is, renounce it, and command it to come out in the name of Jesus. If you feel something begin to shake inside you and you need to cough, sneeze, cry out, burp, or throw up, just do it. Get it out. Feeling queasy or shaky is a good sign. You can secure your own deliverance in this way, praying in the name of Jesus.

Step #5—Prayer of Protection

As we turn this over to the Lord, we need to say a prayer for protection. "Lord Jesus, thank You that in Your death on the cross You defeated Satan and all his evil spirits. Thank you, Lord, for deliverance. I look to You now and pray for the precious protection of Your blood. You are the deliverer; I am only an instrument in Your hands. Protect me and my family by Your precious shed blood. Thank You, Lord Jesus, for victory in Your name. Amen."

Step #6—Taking Authority

Say these words or a variation: "I come against you, Satan, in the name of Jesus. Spirits, you know who I am—a servant of the Most High God. I take authority over every one of you evil spirits in the name of Jesus Christ. I command you to manifest yourself now. I plead the blood of Jesus Christ against you. You demons will not remain hidden or silent. Ruler demon first, I command you to come to the surface and come out now in Jesus' name." You can plead the blood of Jesus by simply saying, "The blood, the blood, Satan, you must yield to the blood of Jesus Christ. You know you are a defeated foe, and you cannot resist the name of Jesus Christ. So, in the name of Jesus Christ, I take authority over every spirit in me. I command you, foul spirit, in Jesus' name to flee from me now and do not return. I thank You and praise You, Lord Jesus."

EXTRAORDINARY SOLITUDE

Step #7—Yielding Every Area of Your Life

If you are feeling shaky or queasy, in the name of Jesus, continue to command the spirit to give its name. Say, "Spirit, you are subject to me in the name of Jesus. You will give your name, in Jesus' name. I command the ruler spirit in me to identify himself first, in Jesus' name, and I command you to come out of me now, in the name of the Lord Jesus Christ." If the name of the spirit comes to your mind, command it to come out in Jesus' name. Say, "I thank You, Jesus, for Your power and authority." Now begin to cough or burp or throw up the spirit. If it feels like it is stuck in your throat, keep commanding it out in Jesus' name. It's important that you remind the spirit that it has no choice but to leave in Jesus' name.

After identifying and casting out the ruler demons, cast out any others as well. Once this is over, you **must** yield that area of your life and personality to Jesus, then command all strongholds to be demolished and destroyed in Jesus' name. Ask the Lord Jesus to take back any ground you ever gave to Satan. This is very important. Ask Jesus to fill you with the Holy Spirit and fill every area of your mind, your will, and your emotions with Himself. Begin memorizing and confessing scriptures for that particular area of your life.

These steps were not numbered by Pat Brooks, Don Basham, or Lester Sumrall. I numbered them myself to make it easier to return to a particular step if you realize something in the process is not working for you. Note that the tearing down of strongholds is extremely important to staying free. Demons utilize strongholds to gain access to your mind. There are excellent books available on the subject, such as *Intercessory Prayer* by Dutch Sheets and *Victory Over Darkness* by Neil T Anderson. Both are excellent sources of information on strongholds.

I was fasting the day I received my deliverance, but that does not mean you must fast to receive yours. The main thing is to just get it done. God made a powerful move a few hours after I was delivered. The thought came that I should help the other inmates in SHU get delivered. They could leave the SHU having had an awesome experience with the Lord Jesus. Most importantly, they could leave free of oppression.

For months I had been preaching and teaching on a nightly basis for my neighbors in solitary. So, I went up to the cell bars and yelled out what I thought the Lord wanted for each of them. I explained what we would be getting into and asked if any of them wanted to participate. The majority were former or current drug addicts or were addicted to some other vice. Most were violent. Three or four participated.

I began by taking authority over the evil spirits. I prayed and rebuked for an intense hour. These men had already been pressing into God and had developed a routine of fasting. One had received the baptism in the Holy Spirit. Try to imagine four convicts in solitary confinement battling against demons in the same place where two officers had been murdered in the hallway in front of our cells. We were in a pit, a dungeon, and this is what we were doing! This is what **God** was doing in an environment of utter darkness, murder, violence, lust, and perversion. Men were being delivered from demonic oppression through the blood of Jesus and the power of the Holy Spirit. Praise God! He is greater than all that sin and can meet any person anywhere on this planet.

What happened during this deliverance was amazing. These men were spitting and coughing. Some were vomiting or dry heaving. I could hear toilets flushing down the hallway as men were getting it out of them. When it was over and I turned from the bars to walk to my bed with a smile on my face, the Lord clearly said to me, "Remember who you work for." That was very humbling. There was to be no spiritual pride. I was now working for the Lord and had to always remember that apart from Him I could do nothing.

Readers, please understand I am not demon crazy. I do not attribute everything to evil spirits, and I don't believe we need to seek them out. I do believe deliverance is important, especially for those who have lived a life in the shadows of crime. You don't know what types of spirits you may have opened yourself up to when your life revolved around drugs, sex, and violence.

We know that a carnally minded man has certain thought patterns that have automatic responses. For instance, he sees a beautiful woman and then he lusts after her. Or an addict sees drugs and he must have them. How do you prevent these impulses and thoughts from controlling you? By receiving the Holy Spirit and getting delivered from the spirits of lust and greed. By commanding the strongholds to be destroyed in Jesus' name. By memorizing the appropriate scriptures so they are ready to be used against any foul thought. Second Corinthians 10:5 reminds us that the weapons of our warfare are not of the flesh, but they are ***"mighty in God for pulling down strongholds, casting down arguments and every high thing that exalts itself against the knowledge of God, bringing every thought into captivity to the obedience of Christ . . . "***

If you're having trouble controlling your thoughts and impulses, you need to learn to take thoughts captive. It is difficult to be on top of every thought all the time, but you get better at it. And you don't have to review every thought, just recognize that a thought is foul and immediately replace it with a scripture. Sometimes it is as easy as confessing that you bring every thought to the obedience of Christ. You can stop lusting as easily as reminding yourself that lusting is the same as adultery. If you're dealing with thoughts of greed, say to yourself that the love of money is the root of all evil. Or you can say, "Be holy as He is holy." When you do this the errant thought will flee. The enemy has no stronghold to hang on to.

First Peter 5:9 admonishes us to **"Resist him, steadfast in the faith, knowing that the same sufferings are experienced by your brotherhood in the world."** And always remember to submit yourself to the Lord, then resist the devil, and he will flee from you (James 4:7). The gates of hell cannot prevail against the Church of Jesus Christ!

In addition, anytime you're having impure or sinful thoughts, or even if you're dealing with fear or worry, Philippians 4:8 tells us what to do: **"Finally, brethren, whatever things are true, whatever things are just, whatever things are pure, whatever things are lovely, whatever things are of good report, if there is any virtue and if there is anything praiseworthy—meditate on these things."** Our minds can only think one thought at a time.

What are *you* thinking?

EXTRAORDINARY SOLITUDE

Between the Chapters

Seeing the Hand of God

Five years later, while in the federal halfway house, I was watching David Hogan videos on YouTube. Gold flakes were falling on the platform where he preached. I asked the Lord for that same manifestation of the Spirit. Why not? I am God's son as much as is David Hogan or any other man who has ever lived. The Lord answered my prayer, and I began finding gold flakes on my room floor! I took photos and have two of the flakes taped inside my Bible today.

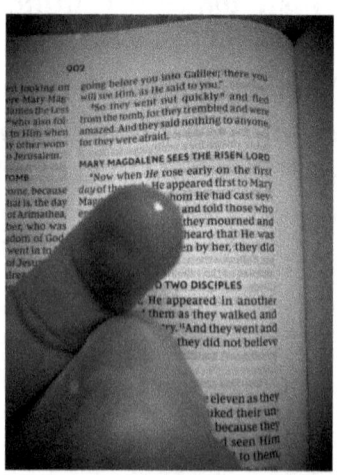

Chapter 13

Evidence of Baptism and Tongues

"The secret is that the Holy Ghost came and brought this wonderful edification of the Spirit."
(Smith Wigglesworth)

It's important that I share with you about the baptism in the Holy Spirit with the evidence of speaking in tongues. To me, this is the only true evidence in the Word that proves a person has received the baptism. This is a controversial topic, and many books containing diverse opinions on this issue have been written. I will focus on what I have seen in prison, what works and what doesn't. God has given me an anointing that allows me to help a person get their faith up high enough to receive this gift. Bear in mind that these men have been extremely sinful, yet they were able to receive when they got saved and further consecrated their lives.

EXTRAORDINARY SOLITUDE

The first time I witnessed another inmate receive the baptism of the Holy Spirit was in Coleman, Florida, around 2006. I had drifted a bit from the Lord and was standing in the day room watching television. A conversation began between three guys behind me. One man, Steve, asked the other two if he could join their Christian group that met in the yard. I sensed the Holy Spirit saying, "Are you really going to let this happen?" You see, this Christian group had bad doctrine. I caught Steve alone and asked if he was serious about getting close to the Lord. He absolutely was. He had just received a fresh 15-year sentence, his wife was struggling terribly, and his son was blind.

Steve had been indicted with Italian Mafiosos. Although he wasn't a "made man," he went down with the rest. At his trial, the government presented pictures of male bodies sawn in half.

Steve and I started reading the Bible together. I took him to the chapel to watch Derek Prince videos on the baptism in the Holy Spirit. I explained what he was about to see and hear and that, at the end of the video, Derek Prince would pray. Steve should repeat the prayer to receive the baptism of the Holy Spirit. He was so hungry and desperate for God. And God met him there in that prison chapel. Before the prayer was over, Steve was speaking fluently in tongues! He was shocked and his eyes were bulging, as I laughed through it all with such joy in my heart. He was a decent guy. I don't know how the rest of his life turned out as he was transferred not long after this, but I know he will always remember that day. And so will I.

The next two guys received the baptism in the Holy Spirit in solitary confinement. Skinner, a former drug dealer and armed robber, was in the SHU for assault. A young white thuggish type with his entire neck covered in tattoos, Skinner had come to Marion from a prison in California. Such a transfer usually meant the inmate was a more violent person, as California and Texas prisons tended to be more vicious than prisons in the Midwest. I had gotten to know Skinner during my first 45 days in the SHU. He was in my unit in general population, and I had witnessed the assault. We got along well enough by talking about sports and crime as a common ground.

We had been separated for about a month, so when he moved to the single-man cell next to mine, he could tell I was a different person. We went to the rec yard for an hour every day and about God. We yelled from cell to cell and studied the Word together. After I read the Derek Prince book on fasting, I passed it on to Skinner. Before long, he too began fasting. He was praying and reading the Word and getting more and more serious about God. He was hungry. God can work with a man like that. I talked to him about the Holy Spirit, and he read some of the powerful books I passed on to him. Even though I told him how to pray for the baptism, he wasn't receiving.

EXTRAORDINARY SOLITUDE

Another inmate signed up to receive Kenneth Copeland magazines. The ministry also sent him a book that he passed on to Skinner. About 10PM, Skinner yelled, "I'm sending you a line." That meant he was writing a letter and would tie it to a string that he would toss in front of my cell for me to grab. When I opened the "kite," the letter read, "Come to the rec yard tomorrow so we can talk. I just received the baptism in the Holy Spirit! I said a prayer in the book I was reading, and the tongues just started coming out of me. It was so awesome! Skinner."

I was so happy for him, I couldn't help but laugh. This man stepped towards God and God stepped towards him. For the next few months, he was absolutely on fire for Jesus. He was transforming right before my eyes. Every man in the SHU could see it, too. When Skinner went home three months later, he was a changed man. He wrote to me saying he had a job and a wonderful girlfriend who was a nurse. The Lord had changed the course of his life.

C-5, who lived about three cells down, was the next inmate to receive the baptism in the Holy Spirit. A former MMA fighter, he was a drug dealer but was in prison for transporting his girlfriend across state lines. She was 16 and he was 20. He was a sexual deviant and was having sex with transgenders. He spent most of his time working out. In the SHU for assault, he had gotten into an argument in the rec yard and had broken the guy's leg. The guy most likely had no idea he was fighting an MMA professional.

As I mentioned earlier, whenever I preached and taught the Word, I stood at the bars and yelled so that the inmates on both sides of the hall could hear me. C-5 could hear the Word being preached, and a hunger gradually developed in his heart. He began praying and reading the Bible. He also read books written by powerful Christian authors. I must say, there is something about reading works by Smith Wigglesworth, John G. Lake, and Maria Woodworth-Etter that inspires faith in the reader.

C-5 also began a fasting routine. That was an especially difficult sacrifice for him, because he was a bodybuilder who focused on diet and exercise. But he fasted anyway. Hungry for God, he pressed in, and the Lord met him there. Like Skinner, he struggled to receive the baptism of the Holy Spirit. He believed he had already received the Holy Spirit and speaking in tongues wasn't necessary. I told him not to stop short—not to believe that lie from the devil. If you receive the baptism in the Holy Spirit, tongues will follow. I pleaded with him not to give up. There was another man a few cells down from me who was telling people that they had already received the baptism in the Holy Spirit because they were saved. It's hard to get a person to an elevated level of faith in an atmosphere like that. You have to fight hard in an atmosphere of doubt.

EXTRAORDINARY SOLITUDE

Then one night an incident like the one that happened with Skinner took place. C-5 yelled out that he had a kite coming down to me. The kite read, "I was reading about William Seymour in "God's Generals." An impression came to my mind telling me to try for the baptism again. I put the book down and prayed. I started in English, but my tongue just took off in a strange language! I freaked out and stopped it, then I felt like someone or something was in the cell watching me. I don't know who or what it was. Come to rec tomorrow so I can talk to you." What a joyful experience for me! The demons in that horrible place were getting ticked off!

C-5 was on fire for Jesus. He read the Bible and every book he could get his hands on, and he continued to fast and pray. When he transferred a few months later to another prison, he was determined to take the fire of God with him. I explained that he might not find fellowship in his next prison—not even in the prison chapel—but that he should seek out two or three like-minded men of God who were determined to press in for all that the Lord Jesus has for them. C-5 left the SHU with God. He took the Holy Spirit and the fire with him to another prison. He was now born again and baptized in the Spirit.

Satan was not happy about losing Skinner and C-5, but the angels were rejoicing.

* * *

EXTRAORDINARY SOLITUDE

There is a pattern for those of us who were once criminals. It begins with repentance—desperate, heart-wrenching repentance. Extreme spiritual hunger comes next, followed by dedication to the Word of God. The final ingredient is fasting. A Satan worshiper once said fervent prayer is the greatest thing a Christian can do. If you add fasting to your prayer life, you will soon have fervent prayer and will be an effective Christian against the kingdom of darkness.

Once you receive the baptism in the Holy Spirit, you need to pray in tongues every day. As these men follow this pattern, God changes and transforms their lives. They walk away on a totally different spiritual plane in only a matter of months.

Sadly, not every inmate in the SHU accepted the Word of God as I preached. A transgender young man about five cells down used to make fun of the Bible and tried to hinder C-5. I asked him to read "The Cross and the Switchblade" by David Wilkerson. He finally promised me he would, but the staff moved him to another range the next morning. He threw a tantrum and tossed all his property and trash onto the tier. It made no difference. The officers moved him to a cell with another transgender. Two weeks later, he was released. A month later, an officer told us that the man had been killed by the police in Washington State. He had become a transgender in prison and went home a broken man. He had tried to get back with his ex-girlfriend, but she called the police. The police drew their weapons on him as he stood in her driveway. He refused to surrender. The news reported that he made a quick movement, and the police filled his chest with bullets. He did not have a weapon. And he may have missed his opportunity to give his life to the Lord by only one day.

Chapter 14

Hearing the Voice of the Lord

"One of the greatest benefits of our salvation has to be that of hearing God speak to us personally. There can be no intimate relationship with our heavenly Father without it. But, as easy as it is for us to speak to Him, the average Christian has a hard time hearing His voice. This is not the way the Lord intended it to be."
(Andrew Wommack)

God loves to speak to us through His Word. He can use a scripture written in a different context and for a different situation to give you a message. The scripture could even have been directed toward a different group of people. But when Jesus gives it to you as a specific word for you, then you have a revelation word and that word is undefeatable.

Luke 1:41 tells us John the Baptist leapt in his mother's womb at the voice of Mary who was carrying the Lord Jesus. I have many times experienced a leap in my spirit when the Lord has given me a specific scripture. This literal leap in my chest lets me instantly know that the Holy Spirit is speaking to me.

In Genesis 50:19-20, Joseph was explaining to his brothers that he was in the place God wanted him.

Joseph said to them, "Do not be afraid, for am I in the place of God? But as for you, you meant evil against me; but God meant it for good, in order to bring it about as it is this day, to save many people alive."

The Lord led me directly to that scripture to let me know that, even though I was in solitary confinement, I was in the exact place He wanted me at that moment.

You may read two hundred pages in the Bible and only experience three verses that cause your spirit to leap, but God will give you a specific scripture at a specific time to direct and lead you. I am certain of this. When I am reading the Word or a spiritual book and receive a leap from the Holy Spirit, I will begin praying in tongues. The tongues will flow out of my mouth so quickly I can barely get the syllables out.

How do you become more sensitive to the Holy Spirit so that you experience more leaps in your spirit? The first and best way is to pray in tongues more often. The Holy Spirit loves it, and the devil hates it. This has been key in my hearing from God.

EXTRAORDINARY SOLITUDE

While I was in solitary confinement, the Lord spoke to me several times in ways some might consider unconventional. God is Lord over all and can move any way He desires at any given moment. As I read the book of Acts, I'm convinced the apostles must have shaken their heads at the unusual methods the Lord used in their lives. The Apostle Paul must have thought, "Lord, a thorn in the flesh? Are You serious?" And Peter certainly scratched his head after his vision on Simon the tanner's roof (Acts 10). God knows the best path for us to follow. We can always rest in the knowledge that He loves us and is communicating to us in a way that will benefit us.

As I mentioned earlier, I did not want to write a book. I knew the Lord was leaning on me to do so, but I was reluctant. As I thought about the prospect, someone dropped off a stack of paper. Then little writing pens started popping up everywhere. And then the first chapter materialized in my mind.

I wrote that first chapter, beginning with the story of my first memory, that of me sitting in the back seat of the car, reciting the ABCs. Those words were still flowing when my friend José wrote me a letter. He talked about how he was making a practice of confessing the ABCs of the Christian faith. Even though he knew I was a Christian and far beyond the basics, he felt God was leading him to discuss those ABCs with me. I couldn't help but connect the ABCs being the first thing that had come to mind when beginning my book and José's speaking of the Christian ABCs. I received this as being the Lord's affirmation that writing the book was His will and that He would be with me throughout the process. God was speaking. We were listening.

Another time, the Lord put me in a situation where I had to lay in my bunk. I woke up in the morning with severe back pain. In addition, my hearing was gone, and I had pain in my jaw. I couldn't work out. I couldn't even pray aloud. I could do nothing but lie in bed. And then the Holy Spirit clearly said, "I said you are gods." Instantly, I recalled a sermon by John G. Lake, which I had read about thirteen years earlier. What did that mean for right at that moment? I opened my Bible and continued reading in the book of John, picking up where I had left off earlier. When I read John 10: 34-35, I understood what the Holy Spirit was saying.

Jesus answered them, "Is it not written in your law, I said, "You are gods"? If He called them gods, to whom the word of God came (and the Scripture cannot be broken), ...

I understood God to be saying, "Steven, I want you to get this deep down in your spirit." So, for almost four days I meditated and read nothing but John 10:34-35 along with Psalm 82:6, the verse Jesus was quoting in John 10: *I said, "You are gods, and all of you are children of the Most High..."*

EXTRAORDINARY SOLITUDE

I read the same scripture in another translation . . . and then another. Things became crystal clear. Jesus said it. The Father said it. The Holy Spirit then said it to me. We are gods! Yes, we are. But we are lowercase G gods. Jesus wanted to be so clear on this point that He said, **"The scripture cannot be broken."** What does this mean?

God is the Father and Jesus and the Holy Spirit. But who are we? We are children—sons and daughters—of God. When we experience the baptism in the Holy Spirit, we begin to tap into who we are meant to be. We are undefeatable with the Holy Spirit and the name of Jesus. I know now that nothing can stop what God wants to do through me. Nothing! This is what Peter was saying when he said we are possessors of the divine nature. Jesus, the only begotten Son of God, works through us His little gods! We should all attain to bring our faith to such a level that we can understand and embrace who we are and what we have in Christ. Only then can we fulfill Jesus' words in John 14:12: **"Most assuredly, I say to you, he who believes in Me, the works that I do he will do also; and greater works than these he will do ..."**

EXTRAORDINARY SOLITUDE

Chapter 15

In My Dreams

"For God does speak—now one way, now another—though no one perceives it. In a dream, in a vision of the night, when deep sleep falls on people as they slumber in their beds." (Job 33:14-15)

"The best way to hear the voice and the heart of God is through His word. Even when God is speaking through dreams, His communication will always be in line with His word. The better you know His word, the better you are able to interpret your dreams."
(Kris Reece)

We must be cautious and wise when trying to interpret dreams. The Lord knows we must be careful in this regard, and I'm grateful He chose to confirm the dreams He gave me almost immediately. He will often give me part of the confirmation and confirm the rest later. For example, God would show me X, Y, and Z in a dream and confirm X the very next day. A little later He would give me understanding of Y and Z.

You can find a lot of material on dreams on the market, some spiritual, some secular. I admit I haven't read much of it. One author might say that water represents people, but could also represent the Holy Spirit. I rely on Genesis 40:8 and Genesis 41:16:

And they said to him, "We each have had a dream, and there is no interpreter of it." So Joseph said to them, "Do not interpretations belong to God? Tell them to me, please."

So Joseph answered Pharaoh, saying, "It is not in me; God will give Pharaoh an answer of peace."

These verses confirm that God will give the interpretation if He gives the dream. In the Bible, those who didn't understand their God-given dreams did not have the Holy Spirit.

The first dream I remember having from God was in 2003, not long after I was born again. In this dream I was kneeling by a lake and tying a bag filled with books to the end of a fishing line. The Lord walked up and stood right in front of me. (I have never seen the Lord's face in any dream, just His form.) He asked what I was doing, and I said I was going fishing with my uncle. At that time my uncle had been dead

EXTRAORDINARY SOLITUDE

for nearly ten years. The Lord told me I could not go fishing with my uncle right now, but I was to go fishing here on earth. When I awakened, I had no doubt this was a call to preach. I knew the dream was from God, and I knew what it meant.

The first dream in solitary confinement came to me during the week I was reading a book by Loren Cunningham, founder of *Youth with a Mission*. He was explaining how *Youth with a Mission* came into existence and how he heard from God along the way. In my dream I heard the Holy Spirit say, "John, chapter 11." That was all the Spirit gave me in the dream. John 11 is the story of Lazarus being raised from the grave. I read and reread John 11, waiting for the leap in my spirit. The leap never happened. I continued reading the Cunningham book and, in the very next chapter, the author explained how his wife got a call from a Christian friend who had dreamed about John 11. She said the Lord revealed to her that He could have healed Lazarus, but He chose not to. Instead, His plan was to resurrect him. Cunningham discussed this further describing a discussion concerning a broken boat. In this instance, God didn't want them to repair the boat; He wanted to give them a new boat.

The Holy Spirit whispered to me, "I didn't bring you back here to heal you. You will leave here a resurrected man"!

And that's exactly what happened. I am a resurrected man!

In the next dream, the Lord gave me a first name, nothing more. The name started with an *F* and was a bit difficult to pronounce in the dream. As I tried to say the name, I kept coming up with "Fernie." When I awoke, I wrote the name down and gave the paper to my neighbor. (This was the second time the Lord had given me a name in a dream. The first time, the person named showed up within a day.) I saw in the dream that the entire range was in an uproar with a lot of noise and excitement in the unit.

The next day the officers escorted a couple of gang members onto the range, and the uproar began.

Once the men were settled in their cells, I yelled out, "If you don't mind my asking, what is your name?"

He yelled back, "Hustler."

This wasn't uncommon to hear as almost everyone in prison has a nickname usually connected to their lives of crime. Most inmates go by these nicknames while incarcerated. Sometimes even the staff referred to prisoners by their nicknames.

I yelled back that I wasn't playing games. I told him I was a dedicated Christian and had spent my time praying and fasting and that I wanted to know his first name. I added that the Lord had given me a name in a dream.

EXTRAORDINARY SOLITUDE

He said his name was Fernando. I asked if anyone ever called him by a nickname (other than Hustler), and he said his mother had called him Fernie.

I yelled back to Fernie, "I'm not sure what's going on, but I know the Lord Jesus is trying to get your attention. That's the name I wrote down. It's on a piece of paper in my neighbor's cell."

The gang banger who had come to the unit with Fernie started laughing and yelled, "Man, that's crazy! You were saying the other day how lost you felt."

Fernie hollered back that he didn't want to talk about this on the range where everyone could hear. I understood and told him to send me a kite if he wanted to talk. He sent me a kite and told me a bit about himself. I asked if there was a possibility that anyone on the street was praying for him. I had noticed the Lord often put people in my path, especially in later years, because somebody was out there praying. Fernie's brother had been recently murdered in Chicago and, yes, his mother was praying for him. I let him know how to get free Christian literature, and he was later born again while still in the SHU. Hallelujah!

In a truly awesome dream, I was walking down a country road and noticed a man in the woods ahead of me. He began walking toward the road, coming out of the wooded area as I reached him. A huge man, he wore a bright yellow suit and carried a bag.

"Have you been mushroom hunting?" I asked. When he didn't answer, I added, "Can I look in your bag?"

"Sure." He held out the bag, and I took it.

I sat the bag on the road and opened it to find blueberry cakes. "These don't look like mushrooms," I joked. He had an earnest look on his face but didn't answer me. "Are you heading north?"

He said he was, and I smiled at him. "It was nice meeting you."

The moment we separated, I realized he wasn't a man but an angel! And he wasn't just any angel; he was *my* angel, the one who had been assigned to me since birth.

I pondered this dream the next morning. When my breakfast arrived, I was stunned to see a blueberry cake on my tray. This wasn't just any blueberry cake, but the exact cakes I had seen in the angel's bag. We had never been served blueberry cakes in the SHU. Never. I knew this was confirmation from the Lord that the extraordinary dream had been from Him.

Even though I was now living for the Lord, images of my former life haunted me. Too often, when I closed my eyes, I would see images of fights I'd had or women I had slept with. I wanted those memories to be erased. Frustrated with myself, I would go to God in prayer and tell Him I no longer wanted the mind of a former reprobate. I asked Him to take this mind from me and give me a brand-new one. Then the Lord gave me the following dream . . .

I was riding in the front passenger seat of a car and Jesus was driving us out of the SHU. As usual, I was unable to see His face.

"I thought we were getting a new car," I said.

"No, not a brand-new car, but always a newer one."

When He said this, I instantly had more leg room and was more comfortable. We drove on in silence, and I noticed the road followed the same path as that leading to the entrance of the SHU. As we approached several tunnels, they began closing around us, and the exits grew too small to drive through. We backed up and went back to the beginning. Once there, Jesus parked the car and got out. I sat there patiently, enveloped in perfect peace. When I awoke, the Holy Spirit confirmed to me that the newer car was my mind. I had been praying for God to give me something that didn't line up with the Word of God. The Bible never promises us a brand-new mind.

And do not be conformed to this world, but be transformed by the renewing of your mind, that you may prove what is that good and acceptable and perfect will of God. (Romans 12:2)

EXTRAORDINARY SOLITUDE

The renewing of your mind. Renewed for what? So that we may prove (or discern) what is that good and acceptable and perfect will of God. Now I could see that I was being transformed by the consistent, day-by-day renewing of my mind. I would never get a brand-new mind. The Lord would transform my mind, giving me upgrade after upgrade that would think more and more like Jesus. We press into this upgrade as we press into Jesus. If we stop the upgrade, the renewing stops, too.

If we continue the renewing process, the bad memories become less frequent and are replaced with scripture, images of miracles and healings, and the peace from God that surpasses our human understanding. And with all that comes joy--the kind of joy that causes a man to dance while in the depths of solitary confinement.

What about the tunnels that were closing? The first tunnel was my transfer being denied. The second tunnel was another transfer being denied. While I was in solitary confinement, the administration had to submit my transfer three times before it was approved. The first two attempts were denied by the designation center in Grand Prairie, Texas.

In the next dream, I saw my youngest brother, L.J., as an infant. I bent over to look into his eyes. Shocked to see they were blood red, I immediately knew they were the eyes of a demon. My initial reaction was to cast out the demon. His father was

EXTRAORDINARY SOLITUDE

trying to help by holding down his feet. But L.J.'s father had been dead for years. I continued to bind the demons, then saw that there were needles of all shapes and sizes laying on his tongue. I wanted to rebuke the spirits, but instead I awoke suddenly.

That night I wrote L.J. a letter explaining the dream and asking him to look up any full-Gospel ministers who might be in the area. He needed deliverance from whatever was going on in his life. I knew from information received over the years that he was into smoking marijuana and partied occasionally with powder cocaine, but there was never any hint of needles.

I wrote my aunt a similar letter and asked if any portion of my dream was true. The very next night after the dream and before my letters left the prison, I was allowed to use the telephone. In solitary confinement, inmates are only allowed one fifteen-minute phone call a month. I used mine to call my aunt.

As soon as she answered the phone, she said, "L.J. is in terrible shape. He's been out of it all week. He's strung out on drugs. It's bad."

I told her I already knew and described the dream I'd had. I added that I had written a letter she should receive in the next few days. After the call, I fasted for thirty-four hours, spending the entire time in prayer and spiritual warfare on behalf of my brother. Three weeks later, my brother sat in church on Easter Sunday with his kids. The initial battle had been won, and the enemy had fled for a time. I told L.J. that his journey was just beginning. The result would depend for the most part on him. God had already made His move, and it was up to L.J. to take steps towards God. We know from scripture that the enemy will attempt to return. It is up to each of us to be certain our house remains clean and full of the Holy Spirit.

We cannot put God in a box. We cannot limit the way the Holy Spirit speaks to us. God fed Elijah using ravens. This is how it can be for sincere Christians in prison who cannot be fed by going to an institutional chapel. Instead, they are fed by the ravens, by their ability to get hold of faith-filled teaching through books, tapes, and divine encounters with men of God. Sadly, there are few available in the prison system. But, as Corrie ten Boom discovered while in a Nazi concentration camp, "There is no pit so deep, that God's love is not deeper still."

God can—and will—reach you anywhere. Just stretch out your hand.

Chapter 16

The Lord Speaks Through Visions

*"When God gives you a vision ...
never let it go, don't let it be stolen,
and push through self-doubt."*
(Karl Clauson)

In Joel 2:28, the prophet tells us, **"Your men shall see visions."** There are two kinds of visions: open and closed. Open visions are more dramatic, like you're in the movie and your eyes are wide open. I cannot say for sure if I have had an open vision, though I once saw something small and black flying up and down the tier in SHU. As I was on the second-tier in a secured unit, it would have been extraordinary for this to have been a bird or a bat. The Bible says our enemy roams back and forth seeking whom he may devour, and that creature seemed to be roaming. During the time I spent in SHU, I saw inmates walking down that same tier, covered with blood from cutting their bodies with razor blades, sometimes throwing feces or food trays, or spitting on staff. And two correctional officers were assassinated on the same day in the 1970s on that tier. Solitary confinement units are filled with depression and fear and create an environment where Satan and his demons can thrive.

While in the SHU, I had two closed visions. Closed visions are like little clips from movies that you see while you are wide awake with your eyes closed. The first vision occurred while I was meditating on 1 Corinthians 2:16, *"... but we have the mind of Christ."* I was just lying on my bunk thinking, "I have the mind of Christ; I have the mind of Christ." Suddenly, a literal voice spoke loudly and with authority, "You do not know what that means." I thought the voice was that of the devil or some demon, so I paused and then began to rebuke Satan.

I continued meditating with more determination. About two minutes later I had a vision. I was standing on a porch and saw a sexy woman wearing tight yoga pants walking away. She seemed to have come out of the same house. I did my best not to look at her in a lustful way. At that moment, I noticed a man walking backwards toward the woman, as if he were being re-wound in a scene from a movie. Then the vision was gone. The Lord revealed that I would be going backwards in my walk with Him, if I were to continue looking at the woman.

EXTRAORDINARY SOLITUDE

After the vision, I picked up the book I had been reading about the Holy Spirit by Dennis Bennett, an early charismatic leader. I read a few pages and had a leap in my spirit! There it was! "You have the mind of Christ." Mr. Bennett explained how a word of knowledge can come in a flash or even in a dream. He believed this is what the Bible means by, **"We have the mind of Christ."** We are given the ability through a word of knowledge to obtain a certain piece of information we would have no way of knowing without the Spirit. The Holy Spirit was the authoritative voice telling me I didn't understand the scripture. But I certainly understood it now! I had been receiving words of knowledge, one of the gifts of the Spirit mentioned in the Bible.

The Holy Spirit confirms all things by two or three witnesses. A few days later I received a letter from my friend José. He started off saying he didn't know why he was writing to me about this subject. He then filled a complete page with stories about lusting over women and the spirits that work to seduce men. Though it seemed bizarre on the surface, I knew the message was directly from God. When a man can see only one woman every four or five days, he would come to think of her as the most beautiful woman he had ever laid eyes on. I thought I was doing a good job of resisting lust, but I still had to destroy that stronghold in my mind and learn to look at women as sisters in Christ.

EXTRAORDINARY SOLITUDE

How wonderful for our God to show us our weak spots. Sometimes the Holy Spirit convicts us. When Derek Prince was in his eighties, the Lord started to deal with him about his pride. He considered himself to be a humble man and never realized he had an issue with pride. At other times, we think we are doing well in an area and don't realize an underlying problem still exists, like a drug addict who hasn't used in a while and thinks he has beaten his addiction. Unless the addict has been supernaturally delivered from that spirit through the blood of Jesus, addiction will always be an issue.

Narcotics Anonymous teaches to confess our state by saying, "My name is Steven, and I'm an addict." A person will always be an addict if the demon who controls that aspect of their personality is never dealt with. When the evil spirit is evicted in the name of Jesus, the person is set free. But strongholds in the addict's mind still need to be torn down. After deliverance, the house—a person's soul—must not be left empty and swept clean. Jesus must be asked to fill that area with the Holy Spirit and His Word.

Once someone is set free from addiction through the blood of Jesus, he should no longer confess he is an addict, as that would now be a lie. Instead, he can say, "I am a victorious child of God. I am no longer an addict. I am a child of the King. I am not a slave."

EXTRAORDINARY SOLITUDE

Sometime later, an inner sense told me I wouldn't be leaving SHU until after another seven-day fast. The first time I had fasted seven days, I dealt with a lot of bodily pain. During the second fast, I felt God's amazing grace. The days flowed by with ease, and seven days felt more like three. My weight loss was less severe, and I felt no pain.

After a few days I asked the Holy Spirit when my case would get kicked back. I hadn't even finished asking the question when He said, "In March." But I received no answer when I asked when I would leave the SHU. Some things God lets us know, and some things He does not. On March 28, the warden told me he had the final determination on my case. I would soon be transferred. This didn't mean the Feds had dropped my case, but that there had been a resolution and I would soon be leaving the SHU.

As I was again meditating in the Word, I saw myself moving down the highway. There was a sports car with nice tires on the side of the road next to a grain silo. I asked the Lord what the vision meant. The Lord told me R & D, the officers who packed up inmates' belongings, would soon come to get me. Soon after, R & D packed my property, and I was transferred. I had lived for 377 days in solitary confinement. This was the best year of my life. So far.

Between the Chapters

A year in solitary confinement would seem like an eternity to most people. While it wasn't easy by any means, that year proved to be the most valuable year of my life. The Lord said He would never leave me or forsake me, and I was always aware of His presence. He was true to His word.

Almost all of us will embody the prodigal son at some point. But I learned that—once you are His—you can never wander so far from God that He will not receive you back as His very own child. True repentance is painful, but the joy that follows is unspeakable and full of glory.

Another lesson learned was that it wasn't enough to submit to God so I could have a ticket to heaven. His love poured through and over me, filling me with a deep desire to become like Jesus. Some might laugh at the idea that a felon like me could even aspire to such a lofty goal, but the Word of God commands us in Romans 12:2:

"And do not be conformed to this world, but be transformed by the renewing of your mind, that you may prove what is that good

EXTRAORDINARY SOLITUDE

and acceptable and perfect will of God."

The only way we can truly be transformed is to renew our minds—constantly and continually. The only way we can renew our minds is to study the Bible faithfully, fast, and pray. The Word of God is inexhaustible.

EXTRAORDINARY SOLITUDE

EXTRAORDINARY SOLITUDE

Part Four
Revelation

EXTRAORDINARY SOLITUDE

Chapter 17

The Door to the Supernatural

"People do not expect to see signs and wonders today as the disciples saw them of old. Has God changed? Or has our faith waned so that we are not expecting the greater works that Jesus promised?"
(Smith Wigglesworth)

My constant prayer is that God will reveal Himself to me more and more, and so I ask the Lord Jesus to give me fresh revelation and new spiritual experiences every day. My faith grows as God reveals Himself, and, as my faith grows, the door for God to reveal Himself opens wider. The experiences I have with the Holy Spirit cause my expectancy for miracles to grow even greater, which opens the door for Him to do more. This is the exciting adventure of the Christian life in the Holy Spirit. We must press in with all our heart.

"... I will know, not the word of those who are puffed up, but the power. For the

kingdom of God is not in word but in power" (1 Corinthians 4:19-20). Paul is saying he would know the state of the Church "by their power." How? Because "the kingdom of God is not in word but in power." We must contend for this power. As believers, we must seek for Jesus' life to be manifested through us. Thank You, Jesus! Hallelujah!

The Lord didn't reveal where I would be going next, but I was confident I would soon see His full plan, power, and timing on display. I was transferred from the SHU on May 22, 2018, and then to Greenville Federal Prison in Illinois, which had about 1000 inmates assigned to approximately 500 cells. Who would God put in my path?

Incredibly, I was assigned to the same cell as Sabu, the nationwide leader of the gang I had been in. We had served time together twenty years earlier, but he barely remembered me. He said everyone thought I was dead. In the decade he had been in Federal prison, he had never been in the same yard with any of his gang members. The administration wouldn't allow him to fraternize with former accomplices because of his status. He had a tremendous amount of pull on the street and in prison. I had somehow slipped through the cracks. Not only was I in the same prison, I was in the same cell.

Being associated with Sabu helped pave my way at Greenville. When a gang member enters a new prison, he undergoes an extreme vetting process.

EXTRAORDINARY SOLITUDE

Prison politics can be tricky and vicious to navigate, even for an old veteran like me. Some men live for drama, and the balance of respect between them is always in flux, especially with "new" convicts like the ones I would encounter.

Most of these men were too young to know me, as I had been in the system so long and housed hundreds of miles away. Sabu had more clout than anyone in the Federal system in that array of gangs. He walked to the rec yard, called a meeting, and explained who and what I was. He told the gangs that I had been in for a long time and had "put in" a lot of work in state prison, which meant I had taken on the responsibility to do the hit that forced three gang members to flee the prison compound. That type of life was something these inmates had only heard stories about. This made my transition much easier because I was taking my testimony with me. As I said earlier, Christianity in prison is seen as being soft. But here I was, a man who had earned the respect of violent gang members, talking about Jesus!

It must be understood that when I say, "talking about Jesus," I let the Holy Spirit lead. In my experience dealing with criminally minded people, if the Holy Spirit isn't saying, "Now, go talk to him," it's best not to mention religion, as these men find it repulsive. They understand con games, and they view Christianity as weak and fake. But if the Holy Spirit gives a word to me and I take that specific word to someone, he recognizes that God is in it, since there's no other explanation.

When I sat in the cell that first night and explained to Sabu all that had happened in the last fifteen years and, more specifically, all that had happened with God in the last year, he said, "I think all that time in the hole made you crazy. You're not crazy are you, Rooster?" And the conversation began.

Over the next year this man would see Jesus presented in a whole new light. He was a hard man who had beaten several murder cases at trial and was currently serving 20 years for trafficking cocaine. A guy like that can smell phoniness a mile away. When you live in a small cell together day after day for months on end, lies or insincerity glare like a strobe light and flash deceit. Over time, he saw my faith was authentic and that a change had truly taken place in me.

The light that shone through me shocked and perplexed him. He wrote about me to his gang members on the streets. At first, he would tell me to keep my stories about the Holy Spirit to myself. But it's difficult for men to resist God. Jesus Himself told Saul of Tarsus, the Apostle Paul, **"It is hard for you to kick against the goads"** (Acts 9:5b). And so it is for all of us. The Lord is ever knocking on the door of our hearts, and it takes an effort to resist His call.

I was still in prison and still a gang member, but I was also a Christian. I had to take all this to the Lord.

EXTRAORDINARY SOLITUDE

This may upset some folks' theology, but we need to stop putting God in a box. He is not religious, people are. So, I take even the most unconventional issues straight to God. He responds through my spirit with impressions in my inner chest, directing me with what I can only describe as traffic signals. A red light means stop and cannot be violated without consequences. A green light means go, and a flashing yellow means go ahead, but this isn't My perfect will for you.

My life after solitary was strange. God is awesome in such situations. He cares about the smallest details of our lives in ways we can't begin to fathom. About a week before I was transferred out of solitary confinement, the Holy Spirit spoke to me and told me to shave my chest so that my gang tattoo would be prevalent. I smuggled a razor back from the shower and shaved my chest in the cell. I hadn't done that in many years. But God knew where I was headed and the environment I would be living in. He knew how I would have to handle these men.

Are you a religious reader having a problem with this right now? Go back and read how many times God permitted men to adapt to their environments. Not just when Abraham said his wife was his sister in order to save his life. In the New Testament, Paul told his brothers to eat what was put in front of them and not offend those they were trying to win to Christ. I believe this is a huge problem in our modern Church, even in charismatic circles. When a missionary goes into the jungle of Africa, what is he taking the heathen? His religion? Is he taking them America? That won't work for any length of time. Take them the Holy Spirit and His power and you have a long-standing work for God.

Look at what Reinhard Bonnke, the evangelist known for his Great Gospel Crusades throughout Africa, did in Nigeria. The same concept applies in American prisons. You can't go in there as a volunteer ministry and take inmates the American-church concept. They already know that. There is a church on every corner. But if you are empowered by the Holy Spirit and give them a specific word of knowledge, or if someone gets delivered, then you have their attention. If we want a different result with prison ministry and help reentering citizens, why would we continue using the same methods that don't work?

Men and women of God need to count the cost. What is it going to take for us to possess the Holy Spirit to such a degree that, when people meet us, they know something is different. Remember the satanic priest who was my cellie? He felt vibrations in his body because of the Spirit in me! That man had never met me or heard of me in his life. That is the Spirit of Life, and the Spirit is contagious!

Chapter 18

Ministering to the Brethren

"God found Gideon in a hole.
He found Joseph in a prison.
He found Daniel in a lion's den.
He has a curious habit of showing up
in the midst of trouble, not the absence.
Where the world sees failure, God sees future.
Next time you feel unqualified to be used by
God remember this.
He tends to recruit from the pit,
not the pedestal."
(Jon Acuff)

After being at Greenville for about seven months, I got a strong impression from the Holy Spirit that I was about to be indicted for the case that led to my going to the SHU for a year. The knowledgeable men around me were certain I wouldn't be indicted because too much time had passed. I knew better because I had heard from the Lord. I began preparing.

EXTRAORDINARY SOLITUDE

Midway through January 2019, I was told to pack up my property. I had been indicted.

I had perfect peace. I know God. I know I am His son. I know He has a plan. It wouldn't have mattered if I was sentenced to twenty more years if I knew it was God's plan for me. My friend José went back to prison on God's command. He had no idea why until he got there. This was one of those moments for me. Whenever someone is put in my path, I consider that the Lord may be up to something. I have grown in my faith to the point that I'm convinced God must be in the circumstances if someone comes to me in an unusual way or enters my life for an extended period.

After the indictment, I was transferred to a jail about one hundred miles away. My roommate was Efren, a little old man who was being deported back to Mexico. After a few days, he brought me a burrito. I thanked him, and he said the burrito had come from the leader of his Bible study and that I was welcome to attend. The Lord was up to something.

The movement in this jail was peculiar. Inmates were locked out of their cells all day except for about an hour when the cells were open for cleaning. The Bible study was held during that hour. The rest of the day, inmates were trapped in a public day room with no privacy. The noise and ruckus prevented effective Bible study. After a few days, I ventured up to the Hispanic cell and met Omar, the leader of the group. He was very young and was being deported back to

Mexico. Though he had been born there, he had no memories of Mexico. He had grown up in Indiana and was as American as I am.

I thanked him for the burrito and got straight to the point. Did he know about the Holy Spirit? Omar said he wanted to receive the Holy Spirit but was unsure of how to pray. That was why the Lord had sent me to this cell! But the jail schedule was impossible and wouldn't allow me the time to teach him about the Holy Spirit or lead him to receive the baptism. A couple of weeks later, the guards told me to pack my property and said the US Marshals were transferring me to yet another jail. I found out that I wasn't the only inmate being transferred. Omar was going with me! He had no idea what was going on, but I knew Jesus was in it.

The Marshals transferred four prisoners to another regional jail, so they could maintain their quota of federal inmates. Most state jails contract out to the Feds to be able to house Federal inmates. This contract is coveted by struggling county jails. Omar sat next to me in the back of the police van. I asked if he wanted to be roommates, and he said he did. The plan of the captain of the jail was to spread us out into different units. I explained to the captain that three of us knew each other. I had been in the system for almost 20 years and, in my experience, it would be more efficient for the inmates and the jailers if we were housed together. The captain agreed and ordered a unit be emptied to make room for us. And Omar became my roommate.

It didn't take long to figure out something else was going on. I thought Omar only needed the baptism in the Holy Spirit, but I was wrong. Not long after arriving from Mexico, Omar's family started a church in Indiana. He had grown up with a church background but, like so many, had been badly hurt by organized church and religion. The trauma had shaken Omar's belief in God, even though he was leading a Bible study. The Lord was trying to bring this man back. His faith had been crushed and his heart was hard. His mind was polluted with false beliefs, and he challenged every word I said.

But God is faithful. Omar and I were roommates for six months. Much of that time we talked about God. By the time he was deported, we had become lifelong friends. As of this writing, we are still in touch on a regular basis after nearly four years. As for me, the judge added fourteen months to my sentence. I knew the Lord had a reason. His timing is not always ours. I was being transferred back to Greenville. Excited to see what God would do next, I was ready for our next adventure.

Chapter 19

Following God, Leading Others

*"If you seek nothing but the will of God,
He will always put you
in the right place at the right time."*
(Smith Wigglesworth)

While I was in the county jail, Sabu, my former cellie and the gang leader back at Greenville, had gotten an immediate release on appeal. I had been away from the prison longer than I had lived there, yet the inmates reserved my cell for over ten months, which is unheard of in prison. I had my cell back within two weeks. Though I continued to be an active gang member, I was also a minister of the gospel. Over the next couple of years, I chose my cellies as God directed. Sometimes I tried to rehabilitate a drug addict through Jesus. Sometimes my focus would be another gang member.

EXTRAORDINARY SOLITUDE

Shawn, my first roommate after returning to Greenville, was a black Gangster Disciples gang member. He was a severe diabetic and in bad shape physically. We spent many nights talking about God and His power to heal and perform miracles. Shawn was finishing up a twenty-year prison sentence and, like many long-term convicts, was terrified of being released. I did my best to walk him to the gates of the prison alive, but it seemed he was trying to kill himself by eating honeybuns and drinking sodas even though he was on insulin injections. Shawn was a standup guy, but the thought of getting out sent him spinning into different moods. No one knew which version of Shawn they would get. But he was always very respectful toward me, and we got along well.

Alone in the cell after Shawn went home, I was able to enjoy my "sweet spot," fasting and praying for a short while. COVID-19 struck, and the prison went on lockdown. The prison created a quarantine unit, and the inmates had to vacate their cells and move to other units. As I had an open bed in my cell, I would be assigned a new cellie. But they couldn't put just anyone in with me, as I refused to bunk with snitches or child molesters. I could essentially choose my own roommate. At the same time, I listened for God's voice.

When the first wave of inmates arrived, some of my buddies asked if I would let a gang member live with me. He was friendly with my group, but I said no as I hadn't been directed by the Holy Spirit. A couple of days later I saw a Hispanic inmate I knew to be a gang member. He was a Latin King, a rival gang, but we had agreed to a peace treaty. On the street we would be classified as enemies, but we were neutral while in prison. Politics! But the voice of the Lord was loud and clear, saying, "That one." I invited him in, and he accepted.

One of the gang members I ministered to in Greenville (2021)

Chronic had his tough-guy act down pat. He was covered with gang tattoos. His organization was responsible for multiple murders in Chicago. Chronic had been in Greenville for almost five years and had transferred from a higher security prison, which always brings an air of respect with it. He unpacked his property, and I could hardly believe my eyes. He set an idol on top of his locker like a centerpiece. The idol, fashioned out of a rock-like material, looked like one of the statues on Easter Island. It sat in a large bowl surrounded by various offerings like candies and prison money.

I immediately understood why the Lord had put us together. There was certainly a spiritual aspect being presented. I started making small talk and discovered that he and his entire family were dedicated to Santeria like my former cellmate had been.

Chronic pulled out his photo album and showed me photos of his mother's home and the shrine inside. One room had walls filled with candles, crucifixes, symbols, and large photos of various kinds. A naked baby doll, which I assumed represented Jesus, lay on a table.

I asked a lot of questions about his faith to see how deeply he was involved. He said the spirit attached to the idol brought him wealth and health and, at times, spoke to him in an audible voice. He claimed the idol would bring harm to people if he asked, manifesting the harm in a visible way. When it was my turn to speak, I explained who I am and what I stand for. He asked if the idol offended me and wanted to know if he should take it down. He was afraid to keep the idol in his locker, because the spirit did not like that. I assured him he could keep the idol out, as it had no power against me.

In a snapshot, COVID-19 was ravaging the prison population. We were on complete lockdown for the foreseeable future. Every three days, we were allowed out of our cells for a fifteen-minute shower. And God's servant and Satan's servant were confined to the same tiny cell. Sound familiar?

After a few days Chronic wanted to know if I thought he was involved in something demonic. I told him the truth: Those things he called spirits were, in fact, demons. He was puzzled. How could the spirits perform positive as well as negative actions if they were evil? I explained that the Bible said that even Satan presents himself as an angel of light (2 Corinthians 11:14). He agreed when I suggested reading aloud from John G. Lake's *Adventures in God*, which describes the miracles in Lake's life. After a few sessions of reading out loud and answering his questions, Chronic asked if I always read to my cellies. How absurd that it hadn't occurred to me that I had done exactly that when I was in SHU with the satanic priest fifteen years earlier. I told him I didn't read out loud to all my cellies, and we got a good laugh. I hadn't realized how strange this must have seemed to him.

But I knew what I was doing. You can only imagine how mad our arrangement made the spirit attached to that idol. Chronic became agitated and the smallest issues irritated him. He made noises to disturb me and sing lyrics from songs he knew I would find offensive. Words blurted out of his mouth willy-nilly. That demon was furious. Within a month Chronic and I barely spoke. He hadn't asked for help, and I couldn't do much for him until he did. He liked the demon and bragged about the work it would do for him.

Taking the risk of getting into a physical altercation, I explained the entire deliverance process to him, giving special emphasis to the blood of Jesus. There was no way of knowing how the demon would react, but reaching out is part of my job as a Christian. Even if Chronic wasn't interested, no one else was going to tell him about deliverance. Mainstream preachers on TV don't talk about it. How does someone get the information in prison where it's so needed? Another month passed, and the demon couldn't stand it—or perhaps I should say it couldn't stand the Holy Spirit in me. Chronic was miserable and moved out when another cell became available.

My next cellie was Ears, an MS-13 gang member. Though we were still on lockdown, restrictions had been lifted enough to allow ten cells at a time one hour of movement inside the unit to shower or use the phone. After a couple of weeks of this new routine, Ears stood at the sink shaving. Chronic, who was out of his cell on movement, came to my door.

"Rooster," he said in a hoarse whisper, "Hold this knife for me. I'm about to get into a fight, and I don't want to have the knife on me."

That seemed a bit strange. "Don't you want the knife in case the fight goes bad?"

EXTRAORDINARY SOLITUDE

He shook his head. "I don't want to get caught with it. Put it in your hiding place."

I only allowed my cellies to know of the existence of my secret spot when I had no choice. In Chronic's case, he had been my roommate during the COVID lockdown, and I couldn't avoid revealing where I kept my stamps, which we used for money.

Chronic slid the knife under my door and took off. I snatched up the knife before anyone else could see it. An uneasy feeling crawled up my spine.

"Something's wrong," I told Ears.

"Nah, you're just being paranoid. Chronic is a standup guy." He wiggled his fingers. "Give it to me. I'll hold it."

I held the knife away from him. "No. I'm going to take it apart." I removed the string wrapped around the metal that formed the handle and placed the blade—an eight-inch ice pick—in my hiding spot. I have no idea why I hid it there when I knew something was wrong. As soon as I stood up, the cops ran in. Chronic had set me up. Having a knife in federal prison can add twelve months to your sentence.

As Ears and I were being ushered out of the cell, Chronic leaned against a rail, sneering at me. We held eye contact for at least ten seconds as the cops took us downstairs. They strip-searched us, then said we would be told what this was about in a minute. Half an hour went by.

Four officers tossed our cell. Another half hour passed. New officers came and went. Nothing. They took us back to the cell and locked us in. They hadn't found the knife! They had looked right at it and couldn't see it! They had torn the cell apart everywhere I could have hidden the knife. They believed it was in the cell and had looked directly at the hiding spot, but they were blinded to it.

Chronic approached, playing stupid. "What happened?"

"Here you go, this belongs to you." As crazy as it sounds, I pulled out the knife.

"I don't want it," he said and backed up a step.

"Really? Well, it *is* yours, and you have to take it." I slid it under the door.

He snatched up the knife and disappeared. When his range of cells was locked, we were cleared to come out and shower. I walked to his cell door and said, "I know what you tried to do. You are being saved by the grace of God because your door is locked. Get yourself out of here now. If you are still here and I can get to you, you already know what time it is."

And, yes, he knew what that meant. No doubt it was one of the hardest things he had ever done. Being an active gang member and checking himself into protective custody like a coward is the ultimate no-no in prison. He would be marked as a "check in" the rest of his sentence. He begged me to let him stay, but I told him he knew the consequences if he stayed. He packed his property and checked in. He sat in solitary confinement for months waiting to be transferred to another prison.

Prison politics being as they are, I didn't have permission to check in another gang member. I didn't care. People were confused, and letters came in from other units asking what had happened. Checking himself in to protective custody was an admission of guilt. In the end, all his gang could do was deal with the humiliation.

Let's fast forward about a year-and-a half to finish this story. I was months away from being released to the halfway house. The episode with Chronic had long been removed from my mind. I never even thought about Chronic. I was on the phone with Barbie, my daughter's mother. A letter had arrived at her house addressed to our daughter even though she was an adult with her own house. Barbie had opened the letter and realized it was meant for me. I was confused as I never used Barbie's address for any reason. She wasn't my girlfriend. I asked her whose name was on the return address. Chronic. He had stolen my family information when we were cellmates. He must have been confused, which was why the name didn't align with the address.

I knew what the letter would say. It would be a typical letter from a typical coward saying he would kill me if he ever saw me on the street. He would tell me that my family wasn't safe, etcetera, etcetera. I

EXTRAORDINARY SOLITUDE

asked Barbie to read the letter. I stood there, stunned, as Chronic's words poured over me. He admitted that everything I ever told him about Jesus was true. He had gone to war with the spirit of that idol and had pled the blood of Jesus against it. After he rebuked and renounced the demons, he vomited up some of the spirits. Others had come out of his bowels in the form of foul, black, swampy water. He had been born again for almost a year.

Incredible.

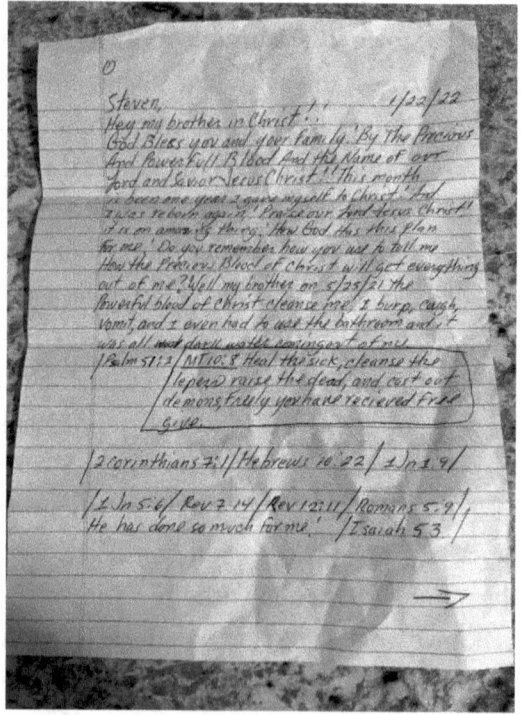

Letter from Chronic—Page 1

Letter from Chronic--Page 2

This is simply another example of God being God. My brothers and sisters, this is why we *must* listen to the Holy Spirit, even when it seems crazy. We have no idea how the seed He asks us to plant will develop. If I had never given Chronic the full gospel of Jesus, he most likely would still be full of demons. Now he is a free man on the inside, praising God. Jesus is King of the spiritual realm; we must never forget that.

EXTRAORDINARY SOLITUDE

Was I clean of sin in this entire story? No. I was furious and would have hurt Chronic if his door hadn't been locked. I'm not perfect. But I have heart, and Jesus has shown me that five of me makes a thousand soft men. If you have courage, you are in that five, as well.

Perfection is not required. Just a little faith, a bit of bravery, and maybe a touch of wildness for Jesus. You also need to cultivate an ear for the Holy Spirit and grow in obedience to Him. That is how we help our society. Do you agree that what the church in America is currently doing doesn't work? If we can agree on that, we can have an awesome discussion on how to set the captives free.

I don't know everything, but I know God freed Chronic, and he was a full-blown, demon-driven man. He was freed because he was given the information that could save his life. When he got desperate enough, he applied the blood and name of Jesus, and Jesus did the rest.

We sing and dance ourselves into a frenzy at church, yet no one gets healed or delivered. Why not? When will our Christian leaders be willing to pay the cost to truly help someone? We pray for someone to get a better job and then praise God for a miracle. That's wonderful to hear, and, yes, God will intercede for that, too. But can we stretch out the lines of faith a little further? Can we solve the issues of criminal thinking and mass incarceration with stories like that?

EXTRAORDINARY SOLITUDE

What impact would it have to tell men in prison that Jesus got somebody a job? What happened to the gospel? Where are the men and women of God who will skip a couple of meals to reach out for Jesus. How about several meals for several days? No, we wait until death is at the door to fast. To say heart-wrenching prayers.

Demons do not care if someone claims to be a Christian. They don't care if you go to church and pray. They don't care. Spiritual authority comes from a life of fasting, praying, and faith. Most charismatic Christians have the knowledge, but where is the power? The doctrine is there in Scripture, so what is the issue? Everyone can identify the problems, but who has the solutions. Aren't we, the sons and daughters of the King, supposed to have the answers?

Provide solutions. Count the cost. Determine a schedule of long fasting and prayer set aside only for the Lord, with no social interaction. Get in there with God and get His power in you. Loren Cunningham, the founder of Youth With A Mission, had heard from God. He had the dream for YWAM, but he wasn't seeing it materialize. He went into a friend's basement and fasted for six days. YWAM is ministering worldwide today. We can do this. If we don't, who will? Who will be the hands and feet of Jesus?

EXTRAORDINARY SOLITUDE

Chapter 20

Answered Prayers for Healing

*"God always was the healer.
He is the healer still, and will ever remain the
Healer. Healing is for YOU.
Jesus healed, "all that came to Him."
He never turned any one away.
He never said, "It is not God's will to heal you," or
that it was better for the individual to remain sick,
or that they were being perfected in character
through the sickness. He healed them all.
Thereby demonstrating forever God's unchangeable
will concerning sickness."*
(John G. Lake)

While in prison, I often prayed "long-distance" prayers for individuals on the street, sometimes without knowing or ever seeing the person. I could write an entire book on the answered prayers for healing I have experienced over the years. Instead, I'll focus on just a couple of instances to illustrate God's faithfulness to those who pray and His mercy toward those who are suffering.

On July 2, 2020, my daughter Jenna gave birth to her first child, a beautiful baby girl she named Brelynne. Jenna and I had been close for many years, so she kept me informed on the status of her pregnancy, sharing everything from possible baby names to weight gain. It was an exciting time.

Brelynne was born during the height of the COVID pandemic. Medical facilities were canceling elective surgeries and trying to keep hospitals clear of patients. The plan was for Jenna to give birth and come home within a day or two. When I called her the day after Brelynne was born, Jenna was still at the hospital waiting for test results. The next day she was still waiting. By the third day, I felt a restlessness in my spirit and knew something wasn't right. When I called Jenna on the fourth day, she was crying so hard she couldn't speak. She laid down the phone so I could hear the doctor report the test results to her mother, Barbie, who had not left Jenna's bedside in four days. The doctor said there was a lack of oxygen in Brelynne's blood in her lower extremities, but I didn't get the details until I spoke with Barbie later. There was an issue with oxygen and blood content, and the baby was hooked up to several machines. The situation was not good.

I returned to my cell and went before the Lord, speaking to Him as boldly as a son can speak to his

Father. I told Him I knew this was not right. That this sickness was of the devil. I didn't beg; I demanded. I demanded the enemy take his hands off my granddaughter. I demanded that the Holy Spirit intervene. I could demand with such assurance because I know my rights as God's child. My relationship with God was not a game. It was, and still is, serious. A man of God must have the revelation in his spirit of who he is in Christ and what he is supposed to be on this earth. I was certain I had been heard.

When I called Jenna the next day for an update, she sounded frustrated but had a strange hint of happiness in her voice. She and the baby were no longer in the hospital. Instead, she was with her mom and Brelynne at her grandfather's house. Barbie told me that the doctors couldn't understand what had happened. They had hooked up two different machines to the baby, and had identical results. When they checked on the baby the following morning, her statistics were completely normal. Either both machines were functioning incorrectly, or something amazing had happened. This wasn't news to me. I had been at peace in my spirit since the night before.

That was only the first time the Lord healed Brelynne. In the summer of 2021, Brelynne had a high fever and constantly pulled on her ears. The doctor diagnosed her with severe infections in both ears. He prescribed antibiotics and referred her to see a specialist the following day.

EXTRAORDINARY SOLITUDE

When I called that night, Brelynne was crying and sounded like she was in a lot of pain. I went straight to the prayer closet, my prison cell. I got before the Lord and took authority over the situation and over the sickness, demanding that it flee in the name of the Lord Jesus Christ. I demanded the sickness obey me and reminded the Lord that I am His son and this granddaughter of mine is also His. My prayer was bold and demanding. I can't stress it enough—don't play when you pray. Get in there and pray till lightning falls out of the sky.

The next day I called Barbie to find out how the appointment had gone. The specialist had been angry and wanted to know which doctor had put Brelynne on antibiotics. Not only did Brelynne not have an ear infection, she said Brelynne had never had an ear infection! The effects of a recent infection would have been detectable. She immediately discontinued the use of antibiotics, saying they could have adverse effects on Brelynne.

Bear in mind that Jenna and Barbie are not religious, and neither will call these events miracles. My daughter cannot stand hearing me talk about God, but she has seen my prayers answered so many times that when she or someone else is ill, she asks me to pray. She has faith in *my* faith.

In John 14:12, Jesus told us we would see greater miracles after He left earth. Please understand that these healings didn't take place because of any

EXTRAORDINARY SOLITUDE

power I have. I could pray and scream and demand until I'm blue in the face, and nothing would happen without Jesus. Our Friend, the Holy Spirit, honors and moves on behalf of a man of faith. God cherishes faith and loves seeing His children move boldly in that faith. True boldness in prayer comes from understanding who you are as a child of God.

"Healing belongs to you.
It belongs to you because sickness is of the enemy.
It belongs to you because you are
a spiritual child of Abraham.
It belongs to you because sickness is a curse,
and Christ has redeemed you
from the curse of the law."
(Kenneth E. Hagin)

Between the Chapters

My beautiful granddaughter, Brelynne, developed bowed legs as a toddler. I received this as another reason to pray for healing. The Lord was faithful, as always, and miraculously straightened her legs without surgery or braces.

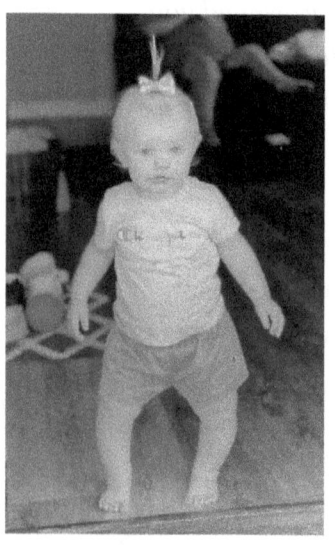

Chapter 21

Led By Dreams

*"Hearing God is not all that difficult.
If we know the Lord, we have already heard His
voice - after all it was the inner leading that brought
us to Him in the first place.
But we can hear His voice and still miss His best
if we don't keep on listening.
After the what of guidance comes
the when and how."*
(Loren Cunningham)

Sometimes God shows up so unexpectedly and in such an unconventional way that we must check our theology at the door. He fed the children of Israel by leaving manna on the ground. He spoke to Daniel, Joseph, and others through dreams, but spoke to Peter and Paul primarily through visions they didn't always immediately understand. One aspect of dreams and visions is that we will know if they are, in fact, from Him. If we're trying to decide if a dream is or isn't from the Lord, it probably isn't.

During the last eighteen months before my release, the Lord again spoke to me through dreams, assuring me He was near and that He cared about the smallest details of my life. In one such dream, the Lord gave me the name of an author and the color of the book cover. The next day, I went downstairs and rested my hand on top of the book return rack, as I sifted through the available books on the cart. Then I realized the book I had been looking for was already under my hand on top of the book return pile! The Lord had directed me to read *Mere Christianity* by C. S. Lewis. I was led to specific books several times by receiving the author and the color of the book cover in a dream.

Another time, I dreamed about a map of the United States, zooming in until I was over Connecticut. I told the Lord that the only thing I knew about Connecticut was that there was a federal prison in Danbury. I awoke to another day of lockdown. I looked downstairs and saw a book titled *Miracles* on a table. The title intrigued me, so I yelled for one of the convicts who wasn't locked in to bring it to my cell. The book was written by Eric Mataxes who began by describing the place of his childhood, a small town in Connecticut named Danbury. Again, the Lord was confirming that He was close by my side.

And then the BIG dream came.

EXTRAORDINARY SOLITUDE

During late 2020, I dreamed of a wall in a home where a picture frame hung. The frame displayed a scripture, which changed every so often. When I awoke, my spirit told me the dream was from the Lord. He wanted me to make this happen. I told the Lord He would have to confirm that the dream was from Him, as I had no idea how to undertake such a task.

Rapha Scripture Frame

I had been in prison during the entire technology explosion and hadn't had internet access for almost 20 years. I had never seen a smartphone or a smartwatch. I had never sent a text message. If I truly was to "invent" such a product, I knew I couldn't take a step without the guidance of the Holy Spirit. I needed real information. And I needed confirmation that this idea was truly from the Lord.

That night the Lord again showed me the product in a dream. A white hand held a small component between the thumb and forefinger. I didn't recognize the object as being a chip until much later, but I knew this was what would make the product functional. I was to create a beautiful frame with a screen that rotated a new scripture every day. Simple, right? But I had no idea how to begin and kept the dream to myself . . . until I was released in February 2022.

EXTRAORDINARY SOLITUDE

Chapter 22

A New Life Begins

*"We never grow closer to God
when we just live life.
It takes deliberate pursuit and attentiveness."*
(Francis Chan)

When someone is released from prison after nearly 20 years, the shock is unimaginable. Walmart is overwhelming. Vehicle rides create severe motion sickness. Good food disrupts the digestive system and makes you ill. And the world expects you to become a productive citizen immediately.

I was given one year of halfway house where I would technically be in federal custody but have the freedom to move around, get a job and a car, see my family, and begin life again. Eventually, I would be allowed to rent my own place. I had saved a little money from the odd jobs I'd worked in prison. After the first few weeks of shock wore off, I felt ready to find work. I started a construction class at a local community college that would pay me for my attendance. However, after the first week, the Lord clearly told me that He would give the product to someone else, if I didn't pursue the development of the scripture frame. I quit the college course and began searching the internet for help. I had absolutely no idea what I was doing or who I was looking for. I didn't know if I had a patentable invention. I didn't know if what I envisioned was possible. But I reminded myself that God is faithful. He wouldn't have given me the concept if it were impossible.

The right people began entering my life. I connected with Michael Stubbs, the Director of the NEXT Innovation Center in Peoria who helped me understand what I was getting into. He never blinked or hesitated when I explained how the idea had come about. After checking my background, he allowed me to rent space in a building that serves as a business incubator. He taught me to use a laptop, create an LLC, and how to think with a business mind. Iron sharpening iron.

After prison, I hadn't known how to make, accept, or end a phone call on a smartphone. I freaked out walking to church. Daily living experiences were new. Freedom was new. In just two months, I was preparing grant proposals and writing business plans—from my own building space. Unable to find an American manufacturer, I used the internet at night and secured a manufacturer of digital frames in China.

EXTRAORDINARY SOLITUDE

I found a graphic designer in Nigeria who is a full-gospel Christian.

Society promotes the myth that convicts who have served their sentences and are returning to society have access to all types of grants and business opportunities. This is a lie. The work is extremely difficult, and the opportunities are almost nonexistent. Without the Lord I wouldn't have met these people or be in the NEXT Innovation Center working on this business. I wish I could connect with the prison system regarding the needs of returning citizens, but they probably wouldn't listen to me. I will try. The Lord is with me, so who can be against me?

Mike Stubbs of NEXT Innovation Center with Steven

The business idea Jesus gave me has become an awesome product and a fully functioning business with a 100-percent customer satisfaction rate.

EXTRAORDINARY SOLITUDE

Incredible! I named the business "Jesus Speaks LLC" with the LLC standing for Life, Liberty, and Christianity.

I have been a guest on more than twenty podcasts nationwide, including "Real Men Connect" with Dr. Joe Martin, one of the largest Christian men's podcasts (episode 714). Dr. Martin told me the episode was one of the best he had ever hosted.

I was featured on NEWS25 in Peoria, Illinois, and PBS produced an episode on my life. My message is the same on every media interview: Through Jesus I have been saved. Through Jesus I have been resurrected. Through Jesus I have received the baptism in the Holy Spirit.

Whenever I am asked for an interview by someone who wants to highlight the feel-good story of a man released from prison after nearly 20 years who starts a successful business with a great product, I agree only if I am allowed to talk about Jesus. I have no choice. Until my dying breath, I will testify to what Jesus has done in me.

I am now the Executive Director of Extraordinary Solitude, a nonprofit organization that distributes copies of this book to places that only accept donations and cannot—or will not—purchase books for their residents. These places include jails, prisons, drug rehabs, abuse victim centers, halfway houses, recovery homes, and certain hospitals. Our mission statement is to provide spiritually hungry individuals (especially the current and formerly incarcerated) with relatable life stories and testimonies that inspire true commitment and the desire for a Christ-centered life. Only the Holy Spirit could accomplish this.

And yet God had still more for me.

EXTRAORDINARY SOLITUDE

Chapter 23

The Longest Fast

"Fasting in the Biblical sense is choosing not to partake of food because your spiritual hunger is so deep, your determination in intercession so intense, or your spiritual warfare so demanding that you have temporarily set aside even fleshly needs to give yourself to prayer and meditation."
(Wesley Duewel)

At the close of my first year as a returning citizen, the Lord directed me to fast. I didn't get an answer from Him as to why, but our walk with Him is often like that. He gives us some of the picture and, when we grasp that, He gives us a bit more. If we are obedient in that, He gives us more. So, as I sought the Holy Spirit, He showed me this fast would be a long one. The longest of my life. I didn't know when I would begin or exactly how long I was to fast. In December, I told my friend Mike Stubbs, the director of Technology Commercialization from Bradley

EXTRAORDINARY SOLITUDE

University and the director of the building where my office is housed, that I was thinking of giving the Lord the entire month of February. Mike didn't say much, and I don't think he clearly understood what I meant.

As December progressed, the Holy Spirit impressed upon me the need to fast more and more. I did a one-day, "warm-up" fast. I had learned that it's not wise to jump in and do a long fast without first conditioning your body. I grabbed the things I needed from Walmart and set my face towards the Lord. Nothing but death would stop me.

For the entirety of the fast, I would drink only water. I wouldn't eat food of any kind. No juice. Nothing containing a calorie. Only water. I am 5' 9" and weigh only 160 pounds. I knew what I was getting into and asked for God's grace to keep me from losing more than twenty pounds. I haven't been below 140 pounds since I was thirteen years old. Regardless, I had confidence that God's grace was sufficient for me.

When you fast for a long time, the fast needs to be pointed; you must have a reason to fast. If you go without food and spend your time watching television or engaging in social media, you are on a hunger strike, not a fast. Water-only fasting is like rocket fuel for your spirit. Before you embark on a fast of this length, please be sure you are healthy enough to do so. The real danger is not in the fasting. The real danger comes when you begin to eat food again after twenty-one days. For four days you can only eat light broths and vegetable soup. No protein of any kind. Eating incorrectly at the end of a long fast can kill you. Consult your doctor.

Who would I tell about my fast? Certain people were sure to notice any dramatic weight loss, so they should be given a heads up. Mike and my pastor should know. It was important that I also inform my halfway house case manager in case I failed a drug test as a result of my urine being diluted. I ended up telling more people than I originally intended, which I'll explain later. This is between you and God. The main thing is to not make a scene out of your fast. If you must attend a business lunch, you can explain to those at your table why you are not eating. You would not, however, stand up and announce that you are fasting to everyone in the restaurant. See the difference? Most certainly you will have to let a few people know, especially if it is a long fast, which I consider to be seven to fourteen days. Anything longer would be a very long fast.

Any fast must have a predetermined purpose. Why was I fasting? I had several requests to bring before the Lord. I wanted Him to increase my spiritual capacity to have more of Him in me to bless others. I wanted the three power gifts listed in 1 Corinthians 12—faith, healings, and miracles—to operate in my ministry. I wanted to experience financial breakthroughs and wisdom concerning spiritual, business, and other issues. I wanted to humble myself and bring my flesh under subjection to the Holy Spirit. I added to this list throughout my fast.

I learned a few key points from previous fasts and from my studies. Stretching exercises are important, but working out vigorously is not advised. Four or more hours each day must be dedicated Bible study and prayer—especially praying in the Spirit. During a long fast you will be extremely sensitive to the Spirit and should pray as much as possible.

Drink water all day to flush the toxins out of your system. Be prepared for your tongue to change colors and form a white film, as a result of toxins being ejected. Other toxins will be emitted through your urine and through exhalation. Be prepared to deal with constipation, which is normal during this type of fast.

The most important component to a successful fast is to be quiet and still as you listen for the voice of the Lord. If you want to hear from Him, you must be willing to be still, close your eyes, and listen—not only with your ears, but with your heart and your mind. Jesus is faithful, and the very angels of heaven are cheering you on. God says to fast in secret, and He will reward you openly.

Jesus tells us in Matthew 6:5-6 how we should and shouldn't pray.

"And when you pray, you shall not be like the hypocrites. For they love to pray

standing in the synagogues and on the corners of the streets, that they may be seen by men. Assuredly, I say to you, they have their reward. But you, when you pray, go into your room, and when you have shut your door, pray to your Father who is in the secret place; and your Father who sees in secret will reward you openly."

Let's look at the parallel passage in Matthew 6:16-18.

"Moreover, when you fast, do not be like the hypocrites, with a sad countenance. For they disfigure their faces that they may appear to men to be fasting. Assuredly, I say to you, they have their reward. But you, when you fast, anoint your head and wash your face, so that you do not appear to men to be fasting, but to your Father who is in the secret place; and your Father who sees in secret will reward you openly."

Note that Jesus begins the same way as in Matthew 6:5, saying do not fast like this, but like this. The same language is used in both passages and teaches similar messages. Jesus doesn't say *if* you fast but *when* you fast. God has always expected us to fast. We are to use this Biblically prescribed way to humble ourselves (Psalms 69:10, Psalms 35:13, Ezra 8:21, Isaiah 58:3-12), to keep our flesh under subjection, and to be able to hear from God more clearly. (See also Acts 13:2-3. Acts 14:23.)

Keeping a journal during a fast is a good idea. I didn't do so during this twenty-one day fast, but I did note the days I heard from the Lord and the visions He gave me.

I began the fast on December 24 at 8PM. I knew from experience that Day Three brings real hunger. Days Four and Five are a little better. The enemy turns up the pressure on Days Six and Seven. He knows you will have passed the days of hunger if you make it to Day Eight. From then on, the physical hunger goes away, and the struggle is all in your mind.

The First Vision

The first vision occurred on Day Nine, as I lay on my couch with my eyes closed. The Lord showed me a pipe connected to a huge pool of water in the sky. The large pool of water is the Holy Spirit that is available to run through us. The pipe is in us and connects to this pool of resources. The Lord showed me that my pipe was about four inches in circumference and filled with all types of gunk. It was interesting that my pipe was bunged up, since I consider myself to be someone who lives a godly life. As I looked at the clogged pipe, the gunk was sucked away and disappeared. I suddenly saw rivers of white water flowing from the pool through my pipe. I immediately thought of John 7:37-39.

EXTRAORDINARY SOLITUDE

On the last day, that great day of the feast, Jesus stood and cried out, saying, "If anyone thirsts, let him come to Me and drink. He who believes in Me, as the Scripture has said, out of his heart will flow rivers of living water." But this He spoke concerning the Spirit, whom those believing in Him would receive; for the Holy Spirit was not yet given, because Jesus was not yet glorified."

I heard the Spirit say, "Now I have increased your spiritual capacity." This was one of the requests on my prayer list for this fast! The revelation was clear.

Fasting clears out the things of the world that occupy our mind, will, and emotions. This, in turn, hinders the Spirit's ability to flow through us and into others.

The Second Vision

On Day Fourteen, I was again lying on my couch with my eyes closed. Notice the pattern. The Holy Spirit rarely yells. His personality is like that of a dove—gentle and whispering. As mentioned earlier, we must be quiet and still to consistently hear from God. That means solitude--spending time alone. That means less praying with your mouth and more listening with your spirit. I cannot overemphasize this spiritual principle. There are literally dozens of instances in the Bible where people only heard from God when they went off alone to be with Him. Think of Jesus going off to the mountains to pray. Think of Moses and Elijah. Think of Peter in Acts 10:9-16. Think of John receiving the visions that became the book of Revelation.

In this second vision, I saw a man sitting on the floor with his back against the wall. He had a black hoodie pulled tightly over his head and face. I walked around him but couldn't see his face. I stepped back and said, "Lord, I can't see him." The man pulled back his hoodie to reveal half his face, leaving the other half hidden in the shadows. Darkness was all around him. I could only see a portion of his face and hair. His hair was stubbled, like a man who shaved his head but had neglected to do so for several days. I didn't recognize him and asked the Lord who he was. The Lord didn't respond, and the vision disappeared.

I thought about this for a moment and then decided it would be wise to call my adult son. I asked him if he owned a black hoodie. He didn't. Had anything happened that I was unaware of? He was doing great and feeling fantastic. The vision was not about him.

As I continued thinking about the vision, I received a phone alert—a friend request on Facebook. I opened the request and found a profile picture that was the exact image of the man in my vision. I recognized his name—Justin (I also knew him as

EXTRAORDINARY SOLITUDE

Shorty)—but hadn't had any contact with him since he worked for me twenty years earlier when I was involved in drug trafficking. I hadn't known if he was dead, alive, or in prison until I received the Facebook request.

The man in Steven's vision

I accepted Justin's request and messaged him asking how he was and how he had found me. He had been keeping up with me on social media and was blown away by my testimony and encouraging videos. He told me to never stop. I shared my vision with him, but he didn't seem too impressed. I went to bed, unsure of what the Spirit was doing.

On Day Sixteen, I went to bed at 10PM. My body ached, and a few minutes passed until I could relax. My cell phone, which was in the front room, alerted me to a call on Facebook Messenger.

"I am not going to answer that." I told the Spirit, speaking into the darkness.

He responded, "Get up and answer. It is your responsibility."

Dragging myself out of bed, I made my way to the front room and picked up the phone. It was Justin.

"Hello?"

There was no response.

"Hello?" I said, louder.

Still no response.

I said hello repeatedly, louder and louder, for thirty-seven seconds. Nothing. I hung up. The phone rang again as I headed back to my bedroom. Justin again.

"Hello?"

This time he responded, his voice bewildered and confused.

"Bro, that is the craziest thing that has ever happened to me in my life! I'm here at the house by myself. I was in another room and my phone was in my bedroom. I could hear this voice saying, "Hello—hello—hello." When I finally got to the phone, you'd hung up. But it was you, bro. I never made that call. My phone somehow called you on its own!" He took a shuddering breath and sighed into the receiver. "I don't understand what is going on."

I couldn't help but smile. I knew exactly what was happening.

"How about we talk about what God is up to?"

He agreed, and we spent a good while in conversation. Justin had been born again fourteen years earlier but had backslidden into his old ways. He worked as a laborer, and no one ever talked about God, only about work, going out drinking, or doing drugs. He was all alone.

"You aren't alone anymore," I assured him.

Jesus wanted this lost sheep back. He was willing to leave the ninety-nine other sheep to bring this one back into the fold. (See Luke 15:3-7 and Matthew 18:12-14). To reach out and touch Justin's heart, the Holy Spirit needed someone willing to obey and listen for His voice. I was that man. I only had to follow the voice of the Spirit as He orchestrated the events that would restore Justin.

Justin committed to go forward with God by attending church and getting involved with men's groups. For my part, I told him to keep his eyes open. I would pray for the Lord to put godly men in his path whom he could respect. Those men would help him. We talked about God's plan for our lives. I told him about my firm belief that the Lord would bring together a crew of former criminals to preach the gospel and give their testimonies. And Jesus would get all the glory.

While I had several other visions during this long fast, the last I will describe is that of the bedridden woman. Tiffany lives a thousand miles away, so we would Facetime. Men of God, like Todd White and Curry Blake, had prayed for her, but she had not received any relief. I had also prayed for her during my fast but with no results.

In a vision, I saw Tiffany lying on her bed. A hand took a key made of gold and put it in her ear. The Lord revealed that the key of gold is compassion and that the gifts of faith, healings, and miracles would work by compassion. I had seen miracles when praying for children, but had not witnessed nearly as many when praying for adults. Though I prayed for adults, I had lacked true compassion. I understand that now. Compassion is the key to stirring up the gifts in me. I will not stop until I am able to use this key to help and bless others.

Many times, you will not see the results of your fast until it is over. Only after Jesus completed His forty-day fast and came down from the mountain did He begin to move in power. I plan to teach on how to hear from the Holy Spirit and position yourself to receive visions and how to know what is from God and what is your mind. The Holy Spirit is a teacher, and He has always been willing to instruct me in my Christian walk. My responsibility is to be a willing student and listen diligently.

As I said in a previous chapter, if you want God to change the course of your life, I believe a seven-day fast would be sufficient. If you feel like the Lord has put in your heart to do a longer fast, go for it. Your life could radically change, and you may get a word from God that will transform you forever.

EXTRAORDINARY SOLITUDE

Between the Chapters

I believe much of what is being taught today in the American church regarding fasting doesn't line up with biblical teaching. Christians agree that everything must be established by two or three witnesses. Yet a "Daniel" fast is a commonly accepted practice. It is the only example in the Bible where a fast did not involve going completely without food. The Bible doesn't call Daniel's "fast" a fast at all. Instead, it's referred to as Daniel's mourning.

Some main-line preachers tell their congregations they can fast from anything. Fast from your cell phone. Fast from your TV. Fast from ice cream. One included fasting from porn. Will God honor this type of fasting? I don't think so. I think it's a bit silly. The world is watching a soft and weak church become softer and weaker. I believe God will honor a three-day water-only fast over a twenty-one-day Daniel mourning/fast. My opinion on this is based on experience and the types of fasting I have witnessed in prison by men struggling to receive things from God.

EXTRAORDINARY SOLITUDE

Chapter 24

Prison, Razor Blades & Jesus

"Men have said that the cross of Christ was not a heroic thing, but I want to tell you that the cross of Jesus Christ has put more heroism in the souls of men than any other event in human history."
(John G. Lake)

If we are blessed in our Christian walk, opportunities will arise that allow us to put our faith to the ultimate test. The following story that I posted on social media logged millions of views in just a month. To me, it was just another normal, everyday story of God intervening on my behalf and His supernatural protection. Then a much-respected Christian elder said, "Steven, people out here never have situations like that. They rarely have their faith tried by fire."

I had been in the SHU for eight months, spending much of my time in a vigorous prayer and fasting routine. While reading the Bible in my bunk, the bars at the entrance way to the tier opened. The noise level escalated as a new convict was escorted to his cell. New SHU arrivals tend to be rowdy because they're pumped up from whatever infraction or altercation led to their getting locked up. I lowered my Bible, looking up when the escorted inmate approached my cell. As he strutted down the corridor, he stared boldly into each cell, making his presence known. When he got to me, our eyes met and locked.

"You're next," he said in a low growl. Known to be extremely violent, Cali was the leader of *Paisas*, the largest Mexican gang in our prison.

The officer continued escorting him down the hall to his cell. I had heard Cali broadcasting that he had a beef with me whenever he was out in general population. *Paisas* had greenlighted me, meaning I was to be crushed or killed on sight. But Cali didn't have a legitimate reason. Apparently, an inmate rumor had been spread leading him to believe I was disrespecting him, talking trash about him from solitary. Sometimes that's all it takes to get you killed in prison. A rumor, a story, a stare, a word of disrespect—all can be perceived as reason enough to end someone's life. Cali had made his intentions known, and there was no doubt he was excited to see we were on the same tier.

Once Cali was situated in his cell, he called the orderly. In prison, an orderly is an inmate who sweeps, picks up trash, passes out cleaning supplies, etc. But an orderly is still a convict, and the other convicts expect him to act like one. They rely on his services to pass contraband between those who are unable to interact with each other.

About an hour later, the orderly came by my bars pushing his broom. He called me to the bars.

"Rooster," he whispered, "the leader of the *Paisas* gave me a bunch of kites [prison notes] to give to all the *Paisas* in the SHU. They're here for jumping a guy in the rec yard." He looked around to be sure no one was listening. "I opened one of the kites and read it. I don't know why—I normally would never do that, but I felt I needed to. He told all the gang members to come to rec in the morning and crush you. They're gonna try to kill you."

In the federal system, you are allowed one hour of rec five days a week while in SHU. You're put in a large cage with up to six other inmates. If rec is crowded, as many as eight inmates may be in a cage at one time. As prisoners are uncuffed, it can become a death cage as officers will not enter to break up fights.

I thanked the orderly for the information, and he continued pushing his broom down the hallway. The only thing I could do was pray.

"Lord, how do You want me to handle this?"

I heard His whisper in my spirit. "Take two razors and bust the blades out. Get one of the long black plastic spoons. Take a battery and the inside strip from an oatmeal package. Put them all in an envelope and send it to him with a note that reads, 'Meet me at rec tomorrow. Here is your weapon. I'll have mine.'"

I was, in effect, sending Cali everything he needed to make a vicious weapon. The inside of the oatmeal pack would be peeled off and connected to both ends of the batteries to make a spark. That spark would be used to light toilet paper on fire. The razor blades would be melted onto the end of the spoon bowl with the handle serving as, well, a handle for the slicing knife.

The Holy Spirit doesn't speak to me in an audible voice, but in a subtle whisper or impression in my spirit. The closer I grow to Him, the easier it is to recognize His voice and be obedient. This is another reason to fast, as fasting quiets the noise in your mind and allows you to hear from the Lord.

I gathered the materials as the Holy Spirit had instructed. When the orderly came by my cell about an hour later, I gave him the envelope to take to Cali. He was afraid the gang leader would figure out he'd read one of the kites and didn't want to make the delivery. I assured him this wouldn't happen. He didn't ask what was in the envelope, and I didn't volunteer the information. Taking the kite, he pushed the broom down the hall. Ten minutes later, he was back at my bars.

"Rooster, I don't know what you put in that kite," he said, "but the dude looks terrible. When he

EXTRAORDINARY SOLITUDE

read what you wrote, all the blood drained out of his face. He wanted me to wait while he wrote you back, but I had to keep moving. What was in that letter?"

"Don't worry about it," I said. "Get the return kite from him as soon as you can."

The orderly was shaken and didn't want to be put in the middle. I promised him he wouldn't be blamed for anything. He was doing what we expect orderlies to do. He returned shortly afterwards with the kite. I tore it open.

"Rooster. Whatever you're thinking about doing at rec tomorrow, whatever beef we have, it ain't worth it. I'm done. I don't want anything more to do with this."

I read the kite to my neighbor.

"You ain't still going to rec, are you, Rooster?" he asked. "I feel like them Mexicans are baking you a cake."

In prison, to bake a guy a cake means you pretend everything is fine and peaceful, and then stab the guy when his guard is down. My neighbor pointed out that the orderly was locked down and, even if Cali wanted to call off the hit, there wouldn't be an opportunity to pass any kites to his men.

"I am absolutely going to rec," I said. "For two reasons. One, I heard from the Lord. And two, God never called a coward to this faith."

Jesus can work with any man or woman if they have a little bit of courage. True faith requires courage and the determination to trust the Lord in everything, whether it's a life-or-death situation or something small.

I went to rec at six the next morning, taking in my surroundings as I entered the area with the cages. The gang leader didn't show, but some of his men did. Once again, God was in control. They never said a single word to me. Truly a remarkable change of circumstances from just ten hours earlier. Nothing ever came of the hit, and it was never mentioned again.

This is the God we serve. He protects His children using the most unconventional means.

EXTRAORDINARY SOLITUDE

Chapter 25

Living the Life

*"You cannot live like other people.
You have a special calling and responsibility."*
(Derek Prince)

As I write this, I have been out of prison a little over a year after having served almost nineteen straight years in prison. I spent close to twenty-four years of my life behind bars—three of those years in solitary confinement. Who can turn such a situation into a blessing? Only Jesus. When you take a step toward God, He will always take a step toward you. Once He does, it's your move again. You must take another step. If we remain stagnant after the first few steps, the enemy will pounce. I lived it. I am speaking from experience.

We must be in a constant state of awareness of who we are in Christ, the benefits of who we are, and what that looks like in the real world—both the seen and the unseen. We must obtain knowledge and learn how to apply that knowledge. That is true wisdom. We must stay prayed up, pleading the blood of Jesus over our lives and the lives of our families. We must receive the baptism in the Holy Spirit and pray in tongues often. We must use fasting as a weapon against our enemy. The victory is ours when we continue in these things and if we will be still long enough to be led by the Spirit.

Steven baptizing his friend, Phil, in Peoria

If you take nothing else from this book, please take this: God is real. Jesus is God. The Holy Spirit is the most important Person on earth. The church in America has misled many by preaching a Trinity of Father, Son, and Holy Bible. Yes, the Bible is true and is the Word of God, but we cannot neglect the Holy Spirit. If you apply the principles outlined in these pages, you will cultivate a relationship with Him. He wants to guide you. Build a relationship with Him, and nothing shall be impossible for you.

Stephen baptizes his niece, Kaisley

If you have ever been to prison ...

If you are now in prison or are about to be incarcerated ...

If you are in a mental prison even though you have never committed a crime ...

If you have never been in trouble but find yourself trapped in a prison of stagnation in your spiritual walk ...

... the solution is not a secret: Apply to your life

EXTRAORDINARY SOLITUDE

all that Jesus has already done for you. If you don't know how to do this, reach out to me through the contact information on the inside cover of this book. I will come to your church. I will come to your prison or jail. I will go where I am needed, and I will teach others how to walk in victory.

Steven baptizes his brother L.J. Together again after 20 years!

EXTRAORDINARY SOLITUDE

Extraordinary Solitude is the story of my life. The stories are true, though many are shameful. I regret that I have caused so much pain to others. Many incidents are spectacular and supernatural. But the point of all the pain and memories, both good and bad, is to present the Good News in a way so that the lost—those without Jesus in their lives—can find the truth.

This book is only a tool. Jesus is the key—the answer—to everything. If the Lord worked to redeem and renew a man like me, He will do the same for you. You are of infinite value to God. Your worth is not what *you* think it is. Your worth is what *God* thinks it is. He says you are worth the life of His Son. He loves you like He loved His own Son.

I pray you will be blessed in the name of Jesus.

EXTRAORDINARY SOLITUDE

*Steven, Aunt Marsha, L.J. & Chopper
Mother's Day 2023*

An entire family saved by the blood of Jesus!

Afterword

In May 2023, I led my online church, Extraordinary Solitude Ministries, on an 8-day, water-only fast. Members from around the world participated. A week after we completed the fast, I was standing at my bathroom sink when I heard the Holy Spirit whisper, "You will take water into tent city today." I had a slim idea that "tent city" meant a homeless encampment somewhere. By noon that day I could no longer resist the Spirit. I had to find a tent city and take the residents some water. I made some calls specifically asking for the location of the most violent tent city. This is the life of walking in the Holy Spirit. No hesitation. No questions or excuses. The answer is always simply "yes."

And so it began. Through an amazing series of small miracles, God thrust me into a homeless drug-addict ministry to run alongside our other ministry responsibilities.

As a result of this Spirit-led calling, we are currently supplying tent-city residents with water, food, clothing, toiletries, and transportation to detoxes. Most importantly, we provide prayers, including spiritual warfare prayers. The residents call me Pastor Steven or Pastor Rooster. There are so many incredible stories of the lives we have touched and the miracles we have witnessed. Perhaps we'll talk about these another day.

If you would like to partner with us in this difficult and dangerous ministry, please visit our website ExtraordinarySolitude.org.

EXTRAORDINARY SOLITUDE

Acknowledgements

I would like to thank my brothers—L.J., who never blamed me for causing his car accident, even though it was my fault, and Chopper, who watched our mother die and had the courage to come to the prison and tell me the story. I deeply appreciate my Aunt Marsha, who suffered sorrow upon sorrow through abusive husbands and three sons who lived as criminals. Thank you to my children, Caylynne, Jennalynne, and Steven, who grew up without a father and yet turned out to be wonderful adults.

Many thanks to Michael Stubbs, the director of the Peoria NEXT Innovation Center, who gave me a shot at normalcy and taught me everything from how to send an email to how to build a business.

Thank you to Karen Smallberger, who mothered me when I struggled in so many areas.

A true appreciation to Ken Zika of Attollo Group, who was sensitive to the Holy Spirit and loaned me the capital to start Jesus Speaks LLC.

Thanks to Jason Parkinson of One Fire Media, whose friendship is much greater than all the free videos, photos, and lunches he's provided.

EXTRAORDINARY SOLITUDE

I want to express my deep gratitude to my pastor, Tom Eckhardt, who's always available to mentor me in the things that prison and spirituality don't teach you, like how to be a husband, a father, and grandfather.

Many thanks to Evelyn Wagoner for editing this book and so much more. Her father went to be with the Lord during the process, and, through it all, she let Jesus lead and craft the words on these pages.

There are so many who helped me transition back into society after spending nineteen years in prison. The list could fill a thousand pages. Thank you all.

Special Acknowledgments

Extraordinary Solitude Supporters

Many thanks to all who have supported me personally, as well as those who stand behind Extraordinary Solitude, the nonprofit organization I founded. My heartfelt desire is to spread the Good News to those imprisoned behind literal bars and to those who are in prisons of their own making.

There are numerous people to thank, including many who wish to remain anonymous. Because of you, this ministry has come to life.

Jody Baker
James Carr
Jolie Danette
Kelly Alfonso Grace
Brad Huey
Wanda Kinsinger
Kristopher and Christina Klokkenga
Kait Martin
Dion and Karen Miller
Armando Negrete

EXTRAORDINARY SOLITUDE

Ticca Robbins
Mike and Donna Sweeney
Jeff Wisner
Members of the Extraordinary Solitude
Facebook page and Facebook group

Those interested in supporting our mission through prayers or by donations may contact me through extraordinarysolitude.org. May the Lord bless you as we are able to bless others through this ministry.

EXTRAORDINARY SOLITUDE

Appendix

Letters to José
(written during 12 months in solitary confinement)

Dear José,

I received your letter today on the ABCs and on living the love walk. Excellent. Once again, the Holy Spirit was confirming something to me through you. Check this out!

I started the book because I believe in my heart that Jesus has been on me about writing. So, on Wednesday or Thursday, I sat down and wrote the introduction. Just two pages. Then I had some doubts as to why I was really doing this. Is it for me? My kids (like you said)? Or something else?

Instead of mailing the introduction to you, I just sat it on my desk. The girl I mentioned that I thought to send the book to never wrote back, so I figured that was a sign. Today I received your letter that started by saying, "Steve, it came to my mind to write to you about the ABCs of Christianity." In the two-page intro to my book, I started with a nearly identical line!

If you believe, like I do, that God wants me to write this book, would you be willing to type it into the computer and save it? Maybe later we'll get it published. I have included the introduction. You have the only copy. Maybe this is the beginning of a New York Times bestseller! There have been a few to make that list that started out as self-published. Read the intro and let me know what you think. I'll start on the first chapter this weekend. And maybe add more to this letter as the weekend goes on, as today is Friday the 23rd. Mail won't go out until Sunday night.

God bless,

Your son, Steven

PS: As for the ABCs of the Gospel, I have noticed that pattern from all of God's generals! Check out Wigglesworth's motto that I read in another book by him. He said, "The purpose of all scripture is to move us on to the elevation of faith where our constant experience is the manifestation of God's life and power through us." He said it was the purpose of all scripture!

I believe love is the manifestation of God's life, and the power through us is the casting out of demons and the gifts. By the way, I recite that and put, "Jesus' life," in place of God's life. Look at Woodworth-Etter and the simple gospel she preached. She counted on God to do the signs.

EXTRAORDINARY SOLITUDE

Kathryn Kuhlman never saw a person healed until she preached a simple message. She said, "I see a boardroom table with the Father, Jesus, and the Holy Spirit. The Father says to Jesus and the Holy Spirit, 'Mankind will falter and need a savior.' Jesus says, "I'll go, but Holy Spirit, you have to go with me because you are the power." The Holy Spirit says, 'You go ahead and I'll come later.'

When Jesus was baptized in the Jordan and the Holy Spirit descended like a dove, Jesus heard the Spirit say, 'Here I am and we are right on schedule.' From that point on, Jesus' ministry is full of miracles. From that service on, Kathryn Kuhlman's ministry was filled with miracles, too!

This is for guys like you and me. We didn't go to seminary to teach people the finer points of consecration. We are action people. Simple gospel. What did Tommy Hicks preach? Simply the healing power of the Holy Spirit. The lamed, crippled, and blind were healed instantly. I love this simple gospel, and you know my brain enjoys being complicated, because of my chess background. But I also see, as you see, simple gospel, simply loving Jesus is what it takes.

Here's a good story I read not long ago. A missionary went to Africa from America. He spent two months explaining the book of Romans to the tribal leaders. Finally, one of the leaders said, "This is all wonderful, but what we need is to be able to stop the demons and curses that the neighboring witch doctors put on our people at night." The missionary confessed that he didn't know how to deal with that, as he wasn't taught that subject in seminary. Where do you learn it? In prison? Maybe. Maybe in solitary confinement through long periods of intense fasting and prayer. Ours is a simple gospel. Thank you for the ABCs. I'm continuing to write the book. God bless.

**

Dear José,

I hope you are doing awesome. Here is the remainder of chapter 5 and all of chapter 6. I like what you sent me about Derek Prince, I put something like it at the last paragraph of chapter 5. I'm still praying a lot. I'm not reading as much, as Jesus has put a burden on my heart to write this book. God has shown me my angel in a dream and confirmed it. My angel is a big Middle-Eastern-looking guy who could almost be half white and half black.

I've been praying for all those people you mentioned and you and your family, of course. I've got to close and get this out to you ASAP. Please don't forget to let me know what chapters you have received. God is moving. Also, who is this preacher, Bill Johnson? Is he in the New Apostolic Reformation I asked you about? Apparently, Dr. Michael Brown is under attack from all sides. His website is, "AskDoctorBrown.org." People call in, and he talks to everyone. I'll tell you what, though, he won't back

down an inch. He said the gifts are real. People are getting healed and miracles are happening all over third-world countries. India too? May God pour you out a huge blessing. Your son,
    Steven

***

Dear José,
    Here goes all of chapter 7. Please, when you write, let me know what chapters you have received, so I know you're getting them. Also, thank you for the $60. You always are faithful.
    I got your letter about Heidi Baker. I prayed about it, and this is what happened. The next day a guy sent me a book about a rock-and-roll singer named Brian Welch called *Washed by Blood*. I read the books sent to me because I believe God speaks to me like that sometimes. Well, Brian Welch was in a group named Korn. He gave his life to Christ and gave up millions of dollars by leaving the band. He received the baptism in the Holy Spirit and is on fire for God. He mentions this prophet he met named Kim Clement. The exact same guy you mentioned in your last letter! So, what does that mean? God is indeed up to something, and perhaps this is going to be that awesome revival. I'll keep praying on it for sure. We have to be part of this thing.
    Now here's my question: why would God want you to stop exercising? That just seems odd. But He is

EXTRAORDINARY SOLITUDE

God. I just know that Wigglesworth and Hagin were big on taking care of their bodies. Wigglesworth would ride first class and tell his critics that he was taking care of God's servant!

José, I think I am ready to start preaching and that when I do the Fire will fall. I've been looking at myself in the mirror, and I even look different. My eyes look different. I'll take a picture when I get out of the SHU and you judge for yourself and let me know. Also, what do you think of the book I'm writing so far? You are about to enter chapter 8. You've got to let me know what is NAR or New Apostolic Reformation. I need to hear clearly from the Holy Spirit on a few things as well. He is so funny sometimes. José, can I see what Tommy Hicks saw? When I lay hands on people, will it be as if Jesus put hands on them? When I speak words will it be as if Jesus spoke them? Commands as well.

Please check on the people you had me pray for because some prayers are getting through! May God continue to bless us both. And our families. I agree with you, my brother, this is huge. What if there are others out there like you and me? Prisoners or former prisoners that are Spirit-filled yet hidden? Fed by the ravens like Elijah? I'm getting ready. God's life and power living through me will do what it is intended to do. Praise Jesus!

EXTRAORDINARY SOLITUDE

The joy in our hearts hurts the devil. Write soon and let me know all the chapters you've received and what you think.

Your son, Steven.

***

Dear José,

I received your congratulatory letter about my nine-month anniversary in the SHU. And thank you for the encouragement. Also, the Tommy Hicks vision/dream was very uplifting. I was glad to hear that he was one of the real ones. As for sending me a book to read, please don't do that right now. Remember I can only transfer with five books, and I have five now. Please, let's wait till I transfer.

Hopefully, by now you have received the first parts of the book I am writing. I am sending more with this letter also. The first part is about my little cousin/brother being born and about Chopper and me going to Virginia and meeting the adoptive old people. All these need to go into the last chapter I already sent you. The years are from age 7 to 10. Just slide them in towards the end of the chapter please.

Today is February 27, by the way. Nothing truly extraordinary from God in the last few days. I did a short fast today, mostly just to be able to pray for an hour on an empty stomach. There's something about praying on an empty stomach. I also think it is easier to receive the baptism in the Holy Spirit on an empty stomach. Both convicts who received the baptism back here had been fasting regularly. It might be because we were so polluted by our criminal minds that something was needed. I know Kenneth E. Hagin wasn't big on fasting, but Derek Prince was. Maybe, like other things with God, it just depends!

My brother, I want to get started on writing and get this out to you tonight. May God protect our minds from temptation in all forms, including temptations of sin and temptations of doubt, which would all seem to be from the devil. My opinion of course. Could be the flesh or the world as well. God bless you, my spiritual father.

Your son, Steven.

P.S. Jesus is alive!

***

Dear José,

Okay, I finished the insert into the chapter you already have. Tomorrow I will work on my 11 through 13 years. The chapters are about to get longer because I remember more as I get older! But hopefully the Holy Spirit is leading the first few chapters for a reason. I agree with you—God must be up to something big! Let's be part of it!

Your son.

***

EXTRAORDINARY SOLITUDE

Dear José,

Today is March 15. I just received your letter postmarked March 10. I'm a little concerned because you said you had received only chapter five, but I've sent you so many more! Please let me know if and when you get all nine chapters. Here is most of chapter 10, with more of chapter 10 to come.

All else is going excellently. Here is something new: I think God is showing me that He may send me to Africa! Now bear with me, I'm only about 80% sure. It's just that He's given me three signs, and the first two were wild. The thing is, I'd been asking the Holy Spirit where He was going to send me—as in what prison. Instead, this is what He did ...

I was sitting at my desk eating chow. I shifted my feet a little, and a piece of the concrete floor came loose under my shoe. I picked it up, and it was the shape of Africa. You couldn't mistake it. Then I moved cells a few days later. We move every two weeks in the SHU. In my new cell, under the paint on the wall, was an imprint of the continent of Africa! It's just like chipped paint under the paint. I asked God for a third confirmation just last night. I haven't received anything yet.

As for the book of my testimony and later about spiritual warfare and breaking down strongholds, I felt it was becoming more of an outline. I actually pondered those exact words before you wrote them. Again, we have to see where it goes. I believe the next two chapters will shock even you! I'm going to start on it again now, and I will come back and write more later. May God continue to bless us with revelation.

Your son,
Steven

**

Dear José,

Well, I went ahead and finished chapter 10. Also, I just received your letter today which included the Mark Chironna prophecy. Wow! Incredible prophecy! Now, concerning chapter 10 ... Brother, it was hard for me to write chapter 10. Some of what is in there is shameful. I am sure you were surprised in a bad way. Funny thing is, I know that, even if you knew all those things, you would have still been my friend. You just would have prayed for me even more!

Okay, please, in the next letter, let me know if you've received all 10 chapters. I don't want to start on chapter 11 and everything that the Holy Spirit has done until I know that you have all 10 chapters.

Everything else is awesome. Still praying in the spirit about an hour a day, and two hours on Tuesday and Friday. And reading and working out as well. Also doing spiritual warfare every day. I can hardly wait to preach. I think you're really going to enjoy chapter 11. I promise you that I will not exaggerate in any way. I would rather leave something out than exaggerate at all. Please pray with me in agreement that God blesses this story.

Write soon, my brother, and please let me know when you have received all 10 chapters. Did I ever thank you for staying with me as a friend and brother and father through all these dark years? Well, I do.

Thanks, your son, Steven

***

Dear José,

Great to hear from you as always. Your letter was postmarked March 14. Today is the 19th. You said you had up to chapter 7. So, chapters 8 and 9 are missing because I sent those at least 10 days ago. In fact, chapter 10 should be getting to you today. Hopefully chapters 8 and 9 show up because they are about you! And the rest of the Coleman years. Chapter 9 is about Marianna and is really short. Chapter 10 is when I really went crazy. I just started my outline for chapter 11. It is going to be like a part 2 to the book, a whole new identity. The Lord showed me He didn't want to heal me, but to resurrect me!

Here is something that actually made me sad today. Trump allegedly said he wants to give drug dealers the death penalty. Just sad to hear anyone say something like that. I honestly can't even write about how sad that is. Guys are already getting 30 and 40 years for drugs. If that isn't stopping or even slowing people down from selling drugs is a lethal injection going to do it? Why not say, if we catch you selling drugs, we're going to kill your kids? Why not? Let's just go all the way like the president of the Philippines! Sorry, bro, I try not to listen to the political stuff anymore. The media could be lying and making the entire story up. Or maybe it was just one of those things he says and doesn't really mean. I'm going to start praying for him now.

About your son and the stamps, that was awesome! God knows, doesn't He? And the dream with the tree-service guys, that is what we need more of. I remember reading about when John G. Lake and his preacher friends were planning to go to Africa and needed $2,000 for the boat tickets for both families. They sat down and started praying together, and soon Lake's friend got up and said, "Stop praying. Jesus just told me I will have the money on Thursday." On Thursday they received four $500 banknotes! They went to Africa and the rest is in the history books. Back in the early 1900s, $2,000 was a small fortune!

Here is one for you. I just got a new neighbor. A black guy. We started talking and I gave him some soap. Anyway, we were both in the same state prisons 20 years ago at the same time. His mom is a Baptist pastor in Chicago. Get this, years ago when I was researching for my appeal, I was photocopying cases and this guy's is one of them! Now the question is, why is he next to me now? I need the Holy Spirit to let me know soon. I never knew this guy in state prison.

EXTRAORDINARY SOLITUDE

I've been reading a Myles Munroe book on praise and worship—it is good. Maybe we will sit down one day and go over the book I'm currently writing. Once I get it all to you for safekeeping and get transferred, do you think you could go to Kinko's or somewhere and send me a copy? Of course, that is a distance in the future as we're only half done!

You have to love Psalms 103 where David goes over the benefits of the Lord. Verses 2 through 5. Renew your youth as the eagles! That is you! Put my little brother/cousin L.J. in your prayers. He's trying to get right. Even went to church a couple times. I had a horrible dream about him two nights ago, full of demons and needles. Agree with me that the Holy Spirit will hover around him and that the demons can't stand the presence of the Holy Spirit and must flee. I'll keep binding them and commanding them to flee from him. God bless you and your family.

You are my family.

Your son, Steven

***

Dear José,

Great to hear from you. The postmark was March 21. Today is March 26. So, you have received chapters eight and nine. Did you ever get chapter 10? That is the last one that I sent you.

Now, you mentioned someone named Todd White, but didn't seem too impressed. I had only heard about him from the chaplain here, but the chaplain seems to like him.

It sounds like it's time for me to start writing about the supernatural things that have happened back here in the SHU. But first let me tell you about this latest bizarre episode. On Sunday, March 18, I had a dream. In the dream, my youngest brother, L.J., who is 33 years old, was a little baby. He had red eyes like a demon and, as I tried to hold him down and cast the demons out of him, I looked down and saw his dad holding his feet. His dad has been dead for over 20 years. When I went to cast out the demons, I couldn't get started because L.J. was spitting up broken needles. They were all around him and on his tongue. Then I instantly woke up.

The next day I sat down and wrote his mom a short letter and asked her to tell him about the dream. On the next day, I was allowed a 3-minute phone call. I called his mom to see if she was going to come visit me. She said she was and then I asked how L.J. was doing. She said that he had been out of it. I mean, really bad strung out. She said she told him to go get help and to check into rehab. I told her I already knew because I had a dream about it and that a letter was sent out yesterday explaining the dream I had. Now, watch this craziness. On Wednesday, the very next day, I went on a fast with the purpose of spiritual warfare on L.J.'s behalf. It was a battle! Just battling all day for his deliverance. No big deal, really, in my mind.

I woke up the next day and had a terrible pain in my center back. And my right lower jaw was hurting badly. It appeared that a wisdom tooth or something was trying to come in overnight. This is the crazy part—I was at least 50% deaf in my left ear and my right ear! Both ears. So, I started praying and rebuking and binding. And it all only gets worse. For four days this went on. Then today, which is Monday, my teeth and back are much better, but my ears are still bad. I rebuke, bind, and pray. It seems to be getting better, as we speak. I just started hearing a little better a few hours ago. What was the point? I couldn't pray in the spirit for hours like I normally do. But I did meditate a lot. Mostly, God was giving me John 10:34-35, so I assume the attack was totally demonic. But now I'm not so sure.

How could a spirit so powerful take my hearing away for 4 days? All I do is pray and fast and read the Word. So, was it the Lord? Honestly, I still have a strong ringing in both ears. Let me know what you think, please. Also, let me know if you got chapter 10 about Butner, North Carolina, Petersburg, Virginia, and this place.

As for the book, the Lord gave me this: Remember the John Wimber book you sent me called *Power Evangelism*? When Wimber was a pastor, he invited one of the old hippie Jesus People to speak.

EXTRAORDINARY SOLITUDE

The guy gave his burnt-out testimony and then said, "This church has quenched the Spirit. We are going to invite Him back!" All he said was, "Holy Spirit, come." Then the Spirit filled the place and the people. The church was not Pentecostal at all. People fell out and some of the members who didn't believe in tongues started speaking in tongues!

So, you see, my little book might just be more like a resumé. This is Snook. This is who he used to be. This is what he says God does through him now. Do we want to see if God is with him? Whatever plan God has for me, no man can stop—except for me. And I am pressing in hard. I'm determined to go after all God has for me. Check out this song by Hillsong United called, "So Will I."

It is Monday at 9 p.m. and I have about 85% of my hearing back in both ears. May the Lord Jesus Christ always bless us with revelation,
Steven

***

Dear José,

I hope you are super blessed! I heard an interesting story on the radio about Billy Graham. Some people noticed at his funeral that his casket looked rather odd. Apparently, an inmate nicknamed Grasshopper, a convicted murderer that did 31 years in prison, built that casket for Billy Graham! He built it in 2007 in Angola State Penitentiary! That is the prison in Louisiana that has started a revival that's been going for years! The casket was made of plywood and the stuffing was from a Walmart mattress. And get this, his wife's casket was similar! I thought it was a cool story.

All else is going great. I just passed the 10-month mark in solitary confinement today! I started waking up between 2 a.m. and 4:30 a.m. to take communion every day. Why not? Wigglesworth used to do it. I am fully convinced, José, that nothing is impossible with God.

Again brother, I still haven't heard you mention the chapters I've been sending. Here are chapters 8 and 9. Nine is short because nothing major happened at Marianna. Chapter 10 will be long. What do you think of what you've read so far? Sad to say but it gets worse before it gets better. Did you ever look on the internet for the street evangelist Todd White? My brother, it seems to me that my time to start preaching has come. God is about to put me somewhere to preach. I know it. I already asked the Holy Spirit when I would be hearing something about my case and He said March. That was 2 weeks ago. I know I heard him clearly.

Today is March 10. I came to the SHU on May 10. May the Lord continue to bless us and our families, as I know He is. Here is a scripture for you—Luke 10:19.

God bless, your son, Steven

EXTRAORDINARY SOLITUDE

***

Dear José,

Today is April 4th. I received both your letters on back-to-back days. I hope you are well.

I had a visit on Saturday from my aunt and her husband and their two adopted children. My aunt said she would have stayed another day, but my youngest brother would be really angry because he planned on taking the two children to church on Easter Sunday! This is the brother I was engaged in spiritual warfare for!

José, I don't think it was a satanic attack that caused my deafness. Derek Prince said in his book on fasting that one time a minister friend of his had been hearing from God to be still and listen. But the minister refused. So, God put him on his back for 4 months. Prince said that now the minister had to listen! I'm sure that story also hurt some Christian folks' theologies.

Now I'm sending you chapters 15, 16, 17, and 18. You should have recently received chapters 11 through 14. Please let me know if you did.

I just read an interesting book by Perry Stone. Please check him out because he seems to be a real rising star for the Full Gospel Church. He has generations of Pentecostal preachers in his family, so please check on him. His ministry is called the Voice of Evangelism. I also recently read a couple books by

EXTRAORDINARY SOLITUDE

Merlin Carothers. The chaplain here loves his books. Merlin's books are all pretty short as well, but guess how many copies he sold of his book, *From Prison to Praise*? Four million copies! He had some awesome miracles in his ministry years ago. So, the devil beat you up in the shower? I remember you telling me something like that while we were still in prison. Did that freak you out or what?

And you mentioned street evangelism. Do you really think that could be for me? I'll pray about it. I would love to be called to a ministry like that. I want to wait until I get to where I am going to write the final chapter of the book—unless God comes with a dream or a vision, which could easily happen this very night.

I did a half-day fast today, just enough to pray really hard on an empty stomach. I mentioned in the last chapter about the vision in February and God giving me a word about March. The warden came by my cell on March 28 and said it would be very fast. So, let's see. Am I ready? I believe I am. But I believed that 4 months ago. Jesus didn't think I was. I'll probably have to start a small dedicated group in the next prison.

My brother, let me get this out to you tonight. May God continue to bless us both. Also, you caught a mahi mahi? Is that the dolphin fish that is green looking? Did you take pictures? Old-timer, you are a true general, Your son,

Steven

EXTRAORDINARY SOLITUDE

***

Dear José,

Great to hear from you. I got your letter dated the 9th, today is the 12th. But we seem to have a problem in the mail somewhere. You stated in your letter that you received a letter from me with chapters 13 and 14. Well I didn't mail it to you like that. I sent you chapters 11, 12, 13, 14, and 15 all in the same letter. Then a week later I sent you chapters 16, 17, 18, and 19 all in one letter. So right now, you should have just recently received nine chapters in two letters. I sent you chapters 11 through 15 over 3 weeks ago and sent you 16 through 19 over 2 weeks ago, so if you didn't receive all these chapters, something happened. And actually, when I got your letter, it upset me because I had a couple issues with the mail when I was sending letters to my friend that used to visit me. I started thinking bad thoughts and then realized I was hurting the Lord, so I repented and stopped. But I'm sure I'll be frustrated a little if you don't get all the chapters, especially if it is because some guard here is playing with my mail. But it is in God's hands. As is everything else. So please let me know what chapters you have received. Are you missing chapters 11 and 12? What about 15 to 19?

Anyway, on another note, I've been submitted for transfer again. It has been sent to the destination center in Texas for the third time. I am as sure as I can be that God is moving to get me transferred. My time here is complete, I feel it. Now I have to figure out how to do my time once I get transferred. I don't want to offend the Holy Spirit by gambling. In fact, can I even play chess for fun without upsetting Him? I don't know. I take all those games like chess and pool and handball so seriously that the game consumes me and my energy until I feel the Spirit is suffocated. But I can't just sit around reading the Word all day or I'll get bored really quick. Yet my desire is to preach and teach the things of God. As you know, this all is a tricky balance in prison.

José, I sure hope you received all those chapters as you can tell it is on my mind. Maybe it is pride. I am kind of proud concerning the book. I know God wanted me to do it, but pride is a big no-no, so again it is in Jesus' hands. After all, no man can stop God's plan for my life.

You mentioned that you have started another book? Awesome! Also, I agree about working out stuff, but we have to do it! Remember that neglecting to work out, bad eating habits, and poor rest equals our early death. Wigglesworth said he was taking care of God's servant, himself. John Lake neglected himself and his wife. She died and left 5 children. He lived to be 65. I think leaving Africa saved him or he may have died sooner.

Most of God's servants in the Bible lived to be old, unless they were martyred. David was the

EXTRAORDINARY SOLITUDE

youngest at 70. But Moses, Abraham, Isaac, Jacob, Joshua, Caleb, and Solomon all live to be older. Maybe I just want to see you live to be 120 years old!

Another thing that bothers me is that I have a co-defendant back here, and he lives in another area of the SHU. I don't hear from him much, but right before I got your letter, I found out that he is having some mental problems back here. Brother, we have been down in the hole for 11 months! Apparently, he tried to throw some water on a staff member, and he just seems to be very stressed. So please pray for him with me. Honestly a year in the hole is too long for anyone, but I have Jesus, so I'm cool. Also, I read this book by Lee Strobel called *The Case for Christ*. It was good, and then I had an opportunity to hear him on the radio. He just wrote a new book called *The Case for Miracles*.

Steven

***

Dear José,

This is what I've been doing lately. I just make talking points. I grab a pen and paper and start talking! Or writing! I don't plan on being an author. I just do what it seems God wants me to do.

Praise God!

Your son, Steven

About the Cover

In the Bible, God often led His chosen through a season of solitude before sending them out to do mighty works. Moses spent years in the wilderness and on the far side of the mountain (Exodus 3:1-6). Joseph was in prison. Paul was sent to Arabia after his conversion (Galatians 1:17). Even Jesus removed Himself from the crowds and spent forty days in the wilderness following His baptism in preparation for His earthly ministry (Luke 5:16, Luke 6:12, Mark 6:31). I, too, spent time alone—377 consecutive days in solitary confinement. I chose the title, Extraordinary Solitude, to reflect that all-important time of study and growing closer to the Lord. My life would never be the same.

A four-inch, non-lethal pen is the only kind of writing instrument allowed in solitary confinement. Unfortunately, these pens are flimsy and uncomfortably thin. To make the pen more comfortable to my hand and sturdier to write with, I would roll it in a piece of paper and secure it with tape made from the label of my deodorant, as shown on the cover. I wrote the original manuscript—and the subtitle, Prison, Razor Blades & Jesus—using this kind of pen. I needed a new pen every couple of days, but the Holy Spirit always provided.

EXTRAORDINARY SOLITUDE

About the Author

Steven Snook was born in Hampton, VA, as the second child to a fifteen-year-old mother. After being placed in the foster care system, he was transferred to central Illinois to be raised by an aunt. His childhood, rife with poverty and abuse, set the stage for a life of violence.

A series of tests revealed that Steven had an above-average I.Q. Though he became the State of Illinois Freshman/Sophomore Chess Champion, he was already on the path to becoming a drug trafficker by the time he was fifteen. After several arrests, he was sentenced to nineteen years in Federal prison.

Through a series of extraordinary events, Steven was born again and received the baptism in the Holy Spirit. He dedicated his life to extreme fasting and prayer, resulting in miraculous encounters with the

Holy Spirit. God used him to spark mini-revivals inside prison, with some of America's worst criminals giving their lives to Jesus.

Today, Steven is a sought-after speaker and has been a guest on more than 30 podcasts and radio programs, as well as a **PBS** television interview where he boldly proclaimed his supernatural experiences with Jesus.

He is available for life coaching, speaking engagements at churches, podcasts, and men's conferences.

Visit Steven at JesusSpeaksLLC.com and ExtraordinarySolitude.org.

roduct-compliance

/2164